£19·50

Catboats

Catboats

STAN GRAYSON

INTERNATIONAL MARINE PUBLISHING COMPANY
Camden, Maine

For Jackie Pellaton

Illustration facing page 1 by Consuelo Eames Hanks

©1984 by International Marine Publishing Company

Typeset by The Key Word, Inc., Belchertown, Massachusetts
Printed and bound by The Alpine Press, Stoughton, Massachusetts

Published by International Marine Publishing Company
21 Elm Street, Camden, Maine 04843
(207) 236-4342

Library of Congress Cataloging in Publication Data

Grayson, Stan, 1945–
    Catboats

    1. Catboats—History. I. Title
VM311.C33G73 1984   623.8'22   83-26440
ISBN 0-87742-162-5

Portions of Chapter 1 appeared in *Nautical Quarterly*, Number 11.

Contents

Acknowledgments

I would like to thank the following people for their help during the course of research that led to this book. John and Pinkie Leavens; Wilton Crosby, Jr.; Charles F. Sayle, Sr.; E.L. Goodwin; Albert Diss; C. Brownell; Walter Zwarg; Mary Schoettle; Gladys Perry; John Freeburg; Sohei Hohri of the New York Yacht Club; John Brackett; John and Laura Saunders; the Wareham Public Library; and Nicholas Whitman of the Whaling Museum in New Bedford.

Catboat men . . . developed an unshakable faith in the boats they sailed. Actually they feared little or nothing in the way of weather. In boats of less than thirty feet overall they ventured miles to sea "sou'west of Noman's," to set the dragnets for mackerel in spring. Instances have been known where such boats, lying to their nets, were caught in easterly gales and drifted for miles before the wind and sea went down, for they would not cut and run and leave their nets if it could be helped.

And when the fall fishing was done, there were venturesome souls who fitted out with unusual care and sailed south for the Florida coast, the Bahamas or West Indies, and fished in those waters until spring, when they returned.

Those things are no more.

—Joseph Chase Allen, Vineyard Gazette, *November 2, 1962*

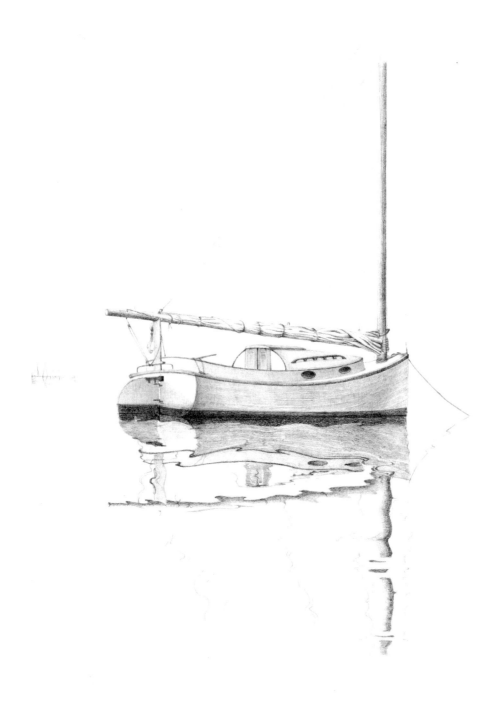

Introduction

A HUNDRED YEARS AGO and more, before there were internal combustion engines, computers, or sailboats with marconi rigs and big genoa jibs to help them go to windward, there were catboats. Nobody knows how they were named, these shallow-draft, broad-beamed boats with a single mast right up in the bow, but for decades they played an important, sometimes predominant role among American working and pleasure craft.

Catboats have been around long enough to have survived all of yachting's trends. They have become associated, in the minds of those who tend to dwell on such things, with traditional virtues such as honesty of purpose, simplicity, and strength. They are as much a part of America's past as a plow or the Ford Model T, or the New Jersey shore in the days before developers arrived and routed the scrub pine and wild places with acres of look-alike cottages.

We know about catboats, in part, because old pictures of them have survived, lithographs of a Currier-and-Ives America that imbue us with nostalgia for a world less crowded, dehumanized, and polluted than our own. There are also tinted postcards of catboats in front of summer resorts long vanished, and fine, glass-plate negatives upon which were captured catboats of astonishing variety. There are paintings, too, sometimes by artists of stature such as Thomas Eakins or Edward Hopper, who was a part-time resident on Cape Cod when catboats were as much a part of the scenery as the gently waving marsh grasses. In these lithographs, photographs, and paintings, there is embodied the same grace and simple elegance of form that remain so attractive today.

1

Nathaniel Stebbins photographed Wapiti *beating to windward in August 1890.* Wapiti
*has the buoyant look of an able cruiser. For safety and convenience, her sail has been
rigged with permanent jiffy-reefing pendants at the clew. (Courtesy of The Society for
the Preservation of New England Antiquities)*

During the years since they achieved great popularity, only to be challenged and later eclipsed by other types, a lot has been written about catboats. Much of this material is thoughts about boats and sailing from men of experience and common sense, men who were often frankly mistrustful of new developments. As long as there are people like these, there will be catboats. While many fascinating articles about catboats were published, a certain amount of nonsense also appeared. Mostly, this verbiage seems to have been penned by those whose ideas were based on opinion or theory rather than experience, or by those who simply could imagine no place for catboats in a time when sailboat design was evolving according to the equations of hydrodynamics and aerodynamics, and, later, computer modeling. Successful catboats were developed from carved wooden models, not formulas, and from lines drawn full-size on the wooden floor of an old boatshop, not a video display.

A certain amount of nonsense about catboats continues to appear today, at a time in which the cat rig has been rediscovered by a new generation of yacht designers. One could argue, perhaps, that the past decade's offerings of cat-*rigged* yachts represents one of the more innovative and far-reaching trends in modern sailing. But these new boats, cat ketches or single-masters, are not what this book is about. They are not what traditional catboats are about, either. These are sailing machines possessing sophisticated high-tech rigs and sails sometimes controlled by a dozen lines or more. They are thoroughly modern creations with fin or modified full keels and, usually, highly stylized topsides. They have nothing more in common with a gaff-rigged catboat than their absence of headsails.

This book is about *real* catboats, the sort of broad-beamed, centerboard boat that remains the same in its essentials today as it was a century or more ago. It is about the people who designed those boats and built them, and it is about those who sail catboats today. They are people somehow out of step with the rest of the sailing world. A few of them may wonder whether the rest of the world will ever *catch up* to them. Most don't care. They are not bothered by the lack of glossy, four-color advertising for catboats in the latest sailing magazines. No amount of verbiage penned by a copywriter and attractively packaged by a graphics designer could ever change their idea about what makes a wholesome, handsome boat, or alter their simple philosophy of sailing.

Catboat people tend to be individualistic without being aggressively opinionated. Most came to the conclusion, a long time ago, that a cruising boat does not need more than one sail to be fun or efficient. They have long since forgotten about achieving the last degree of windward ability, finding it more important to be able to reach really shallow water—not the four- or five-foot depth made accessible by the "shoal-draft" boat of some advertisement—and there find a peaceful, quiet anchorage away from the ever-growing crowds of new boat owners.

Many of these sailors carry within them an abiding respect for the ways of the past and an admiration for a more self-sufficient, independent generation of yachtsmen and fishermen. There are few men now living who experienced sailing or racing aboard one of the great catboats built in the classic era of the type, which began in the mid- to late 1880s and ended shortly after World War I. There are equally few who once got their living aboard the catboats that were so common in the country's coastwise fisheries. But the sturdy spirit of those people and their boats lives on, if in a modest way. I hope the following chapters will show how, and why.

1

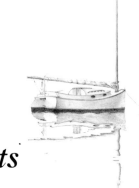

Catboats

BEFORE THE PILGRIMS CAME, and for some years thereafter, the place bore the name the Mashpee Indians had given it—Cotocheset. One May day in 1648, a Mashpee chief named Paupmumuck puffed a pipe of peace with a rugged, red-haired old Pilgrim named Myles Standish, and Cotocheset, with its woods, ponds, bays, and islands, became a part of Barnstable. The price was three brass kettles, a bushel of corn, and hunting and fishing rights. After a while, Cotocheset came to be known as "Lowell's neighborhood," and then, when the nearby bays began to yield their abundance of oysters, the town that had grown up there was called Oysterville. Today, it is Osterville.

Although people began summering in Osterville in the mid-1860s, the village has remained aloof from the frenzied commercial activity that energizes some of its neighbors. Except for a comparatively few shops and an historical society open two afternoons a week, there is little to attract the vacationing crowds that overrun much of Cape Cod. But to those involved with catboats, the village exerts a not-quite-mystical attraction. Catboat builders once plied their craft in many places—both on and off the Cape—but only Osterville was home to the Crosbys.

For a hundred years, roughly between 1835 and 1935, successive Crosby generations became boatbuilders, and during much of that period these same Crosbys designed and built Cape Cod catboats. Three-quarters of a century ago, when *The Rudder* magazine published a story about the Crosbys' boats, Osterville was cited as the place "where the Cape cats breed."

Out behind the Osterville Historical Society is an old cedar-shingled building with a carved sign above the doorway. Painted blue with gold letters, this sign reads, "Boat House." Gathered there is an assortment of tools once used by the Crosbys and by other local boatbuilders. There is, in addition, a collection of memorabilia and old photographs tracing the legend of the Cape Cod catboat. The collection shows fishing catboats and racing catboats and a catboat called *On Time*, aboard which are 25 young ladies in summery skirts and blouses, apparently poised to embark on a day's sail. There is a portrait or two of the Crosbys themselves and their workmen. Most are wearing hats or caps and vests, as was the custom many years ago. On display, too, is a partly completed hull. In the little Boat House, illuminated by dust-filtered sunlight, the hull's ribs and stringers contrive to look somehow prehistoric, like Mesozoic dinosaur bones.

Hanging on a wall not far from the hull is a letter written by H. Manley Crosby. It relates the sole, more-or-less-authenticated tale of how the catboat got its name. According to the letter, it was Horace Crosby who, in 1850, built a 14-footer named *Little Eva* that had a centerboard, a mast stepped right in the bow, and, Horace Crosby said, the quickness of a cat. It is only fair to add that similar statements have been attributed to others and that the date itself is open to conjecture. Little Eva was a character in Harriet Beecher Stowe's *Uncle Tom's Cabin*, published first in 1852, two years *after* Horace Crosby launched his boat. But the fact remains: Nobody has come up with a better version of how the catboat got its name.

The last Crosby catboat but one ever built was completed in 1968. She is in most ways identical to the 20-foot 10-inch Crosby cat on display at Mystic Seaport, and she carries the same name, *Frances*. The original *Frances* was designed by Wilton Crosby and built in 1900 for a Nantucket family. Her namesake was built by Wilton Crosby, Jr., for Townsend Hornor of Osterville. Hornor grew up around catboats and retains an enduring affection for them, not to mention an impressive collection of catboat half-models and paintings.

He is an affable, outgoing man, and once each summer, he and his family host a gathering of catboat devotees. In 1979, the first time I attended Hornor's rendezvous, some 100 people had gathered, and *Frances* was surrounded on her mooring by two dozen other catboats. It was a rainy weekend. Black and gray clouds quilted Cape Cod and Nantucket Sound, but the catboat skippers decided to make their annual excursion anyway. Soon West Bay was dotted with big gaff-headed sails filling with a light breeze.

Frances's sail is embellished with the words, Osterville Free Library, a bit of advertising suggested by Hornor, whose energetic wife, Betsy, is president of the library board. Such messages sewn upon catboat sails have ample precedent. As late as the 1920s, working catboats from New England to Atlantic City carried sails promoting everything from water to restaurants, hardware, baked goods, bonbons, and jewelers. Once underway, *Frances* heeled slightly, leading a gentle parade into North Bay, past the shops where earlier generations of Crosbys once built their boats, about 35 a year, year after year, until they had made some 3,500 of various types. Boats still are built in these yards on occasion, but not catboats.

As the fleet moved up Cotuit Bay, informal races began, and centerboards were quickly raised and lowered as boats tacked into and out of shoal water. There was a rippling chorus of happy laughs as the catboats, in light air, slipped past a modern red-hulled sloop festooned with racing gear.

Shown at anchor in Osterville are a few of the boats attending a Catboat Association rendezvous. Cygnet, *the 26-footer in the foreground, was built in the Crosby shops in 1931. Rafted to her is* Tambourine, *a 21-footer built by Bud McIntosh in 1959 to a Fenwick Williams design. Just ahead of them, with the short cabin and large cockpit of a workboat, is* Vanity, *built by Manuel Swartz Roberts in Edgartown in 1929. (Stan Grayson photo)*

"I love it when we pass those things," said one skipper's wife. "Hey," she yelled, "get a catboat!" The crew of the sloop smiled and waved. They appeared mystified to find themselves surrounded by a fleet of gaff-rigged relics, but willing to enjoy the spectacle anyway.

There was a hint of sunshine as the catboats maneuvered single file into the narrow, winding channel leading from Cotuit Bay into the Seapuit River. The sun sparkled on the gray water and turned the beach grass on the white dunes a bright green. Coming out of the river, the catboat skippers trimmed their sheets and reached past Osterville Grand Island, once a source of timber for the Crosbys, and back to their anchorage off the Hornors' dock. That night, there was a cookout. The sailors, most of them members of a congenial extended family called The Catboat Association, made new friends and exchanged addresses. In common with other groups or clubs, the membership comes from diverse backgrounds but shares a

Almira undergoes sea trials in May 1890, not long after she was launched by C.C. Hanley. The builder considered her among his very best efforts, and she was still a dominating force in catboat racing a quarter of a century after this photograph was taken. (Nathaniel L. Stebbins photo. Courtesy of The Society for the Preservation of New England Antiquities)

mutual interest, in this case an apparently insatiable curiosity about everything pertaining to the construction, maintenance, use, and general lore of catboats.

"We really get a bit *loony* about this sometimes," one said.

"Look at that," said another wistfully to his wife. He had a white plastic fork in his hand and was pointing it at the anchored catboats. "That's just what it must have looked like around here a hundred years ago," he told her. "But now the old boys are gone and it's up to us to remember and keep it going." Then he turned his attention back to his burger and salad.

I never thought I would ever meet one of the "old boys," but I did. I learned of him quite accidentally one day at the Quincy Historical Society. Having pursued my research about C.C. Hanley, the great Quincy boatbuilder, I speculated aloud to the Society's historian that there was nobody around anymore who really had known C.C. Hanley.

Mudjekeewis, *built during the winter of 1889-90 by Daniel and C.H. Crosby, is shown* (**top**) *in racing trim that summer. In her first season she won the championship of the Dorchester Yacht Club.* Mudjekeewis *earned a reputation for being slow in light air and difficult to handle off the wind, but she was, by all reports, a superb windward performer. She was heavily built for racing, and her centerboard was placed off center to make for a stronger keel. Her imposing original rig included a 40-foot mast, a 39-foot 6-inch boom, and a 27-foot gaff. William Whitmarsh, her first owner, believed that she was oversparred and might have won more races if skippered and crewed by professionals. Her rig was later reduced for cruising. Her small cockpit crowded with daysailors, she is shown* (**above**) *with her smaller main, which needed four rather than five sets of reef points and did not extend to the end of the boom. Note that blocks were fitted to the boom and mast to gain advantage for the topping lift. (Nathaniel L. Stebbins photos. Courtesy of The Society for the Preservation of New England Antiquities)*

"Oh yes there is," said H. Hobart Holly. "He lives across the street and around the corner."

Barely able to believe my good fortune, I made a phone call and hurried out. The old man was sitting in the bay window of his living room, watching a squirrel, it seemed, when I showed up. He opened the door for me and then shuffled rather quickly back to his seat, indicating to me the ancient chair that faced his. His name was C. Willis Garey, and he was 90 years old. When he was an adolescent, he had sailed often aboard one of the greatest racing catboats ever built, C.C. Hanley's *Almira*. "I singlehanded her a hundred times," he said of the 25-foot boat, which then carried 950 square feet of sail, "and in races I was always on the centerboard. I weighed 98 pounds then."

The room in which we sat was decorated with framed photographs Garey had taken 70 years earlier. An avid photographer, he had wielded a view camera as if it were a 35 millimeter. There was Boston's now-vanished T Wharf in 1913, crowded with lively fishing schooners. Here were many famous racing catboats competing in Boston Harbor before the Great War. In the 1890s, when he was born, Garey said he guessed half the small craft in the harbor were probably catboats.

He remembers *Almira* particularly, of course, and in awesome detail. "Her centerboard was 1½-inch oak. Her planking was ⅝-inch North Carolina pine. Her mast was 18 inches behind the bow. She was built to the 25-foot-waterline rule, one reason for an underhung (rather than a barndoor) rudder. In 1916, Dr. Jones [the dentist who then owned *Almira*] took her back to Hanley. He put a 2,300-pound seven-inch-deep lead keel on her, running from forward of the centerboard back to the rudder. We drew three feet board up and 7½ feet board down. In 1916 we had 31 races for seven boats and won 19. She always went to windward better than anybody. Dr. Jones put melted lard on her bottom to help her go."

Of the seven catboats that participated in these races, four were built by Hanley, whom a yachting journalist once called "the master of shoal draft." These four boats were *Almira*, *Iris*, *Dartwell*, and *Clara*. The other three boats—*Dolly*, *Mudjekeewis*, and *Grayling*—were not built by C.C. Hanley. They were built by the Crosbys.

Horace S. Crosby and his father, Andrew, began building boats at Osterville in 1835. Horace was nine years old. These were not catboats, and speculation about the catboat's origin is little more precise than that regarding the derivation of the name itself. The only source Andrew Crosby ever claimed for his idea of a centerboard boat with a single sail and a mast stepped in the bow was spiritual. He had a *vision*, it seems. This vision was unrequited and the first Crosby catboat was still unbuilt when Andrew died, apparently in 1850. It remained for Horace, then 24, to continue the craft's development. He was assisted by his younger brother Charles Worthington Crosby.

"When difficulties arose on which the young men needed help, Tirza, their mother, would hold a 'seance' and bring them advice from their father on their mistakes and how to remedy them." That is the tale behind *Little Eva* as recorded by Donald Payson in his *Barnstable, Three Centuries of a Cape Cod Town*. Horace, perhaps, had little sympathy for the story. He told his son Manley that the first catboat *he* had ever seen was not in a dream, but in Narragansett Bay.

L. Francis Herreshoff believed the catboat originated in Newport in colonial times. His father, Nathanael, had sketched for him pictures of the Point boats—so-called because they were built on a spit of land in Newport Harbor. These were keel boats with a mast well forward and a single sail. Nathanael also showed his sketch to Howard Chapelle, who typically pursued the question of the catboat's origin to somewhat greater lengths, though still inconclusively.

"The history of the American catboat previous to 1850 is a matter of conjecture," Chapelle wrote in 1936, "even the source of the name being shrouded in mystery. It is commonly believed that the cat is a descendant of some early Dutch type, but it is far more likely that the cat is a modification of the old centerboard sloops of the 40's, so common in New York waters in those days. These sloops were designed to work under mainsail alone, when desirable, so it was natural that a type should evolve that would require no headsail."

Chapelle thought that the catboat came into being some time before 1855 in several regions: Cape Cod and Massachusetts Bay, Narragansett Bay, Long Island Sound, and Barnegat Bay. These are the waters, together with Great South Bay and a scattering of other places, where catboats were used for work and later for pleasure. Chapelle's theories are as reasonable as any of those one is likely to study, but the fact remains that the boats' background or date of conception will always remain enigmatic. Even William P. Stephens, dean of America's yachting historians, was stumped by the mystery of the catboat. "It is impossible to say when and how it originated," he wrote in the late 1800s. "It is apparently a spontaneous growth called forth by certain needs and certain fixed conditions."

There seems no real reason to doubt that craft bearing some resemblance to the wide, shallow-draft boats with a single sail set on a mast in the bow existed around New Jersey and New York as early as the late 1700s, as some have claimed. The earliest example of the general type of which any specific information survives was *Una*. She was a cat-rigged, 16½-foot centerboard boat built in what is now Bayonne, New Jersey, in 1852 by Robert Fish. By 1852, Bob Fish had firmly established his reputation as an oysterman, boatbuilder, and skipper of everything from fast racing sandbaggers to large sloops and schooners. *Una* was shipped to England, apparently as a gift to a gentleman who bore the title Marquis of Conyngham. The Marquis launched *Una* right in Hyde Park, on the Serpentine, where one may still rent a small sailing dinghy or rowing boat. *Una*'s simplicity, speed, and general handiness in reasonably smooth water impressed all who sailed her, including, it seems, the Prince of Wales. She was still afloat 40 years after her first sail, and she prompted a number of copies and larger versions, referred to by the British as Unaboats or, occasionally, Bob Fish boats. Beken photographed one of them, *Vigia*, slicing neatly through the water off Harwich, Essex, a British ensign at her peak.

Una, with her 6½-foot beam and nine-inch draft, was both narrower and rather more shallow than the catboats that subsequently developed. These possessed not merely a cat rig but that peculiar combination of rig and hull form that constitutes a "true" catboat. The term implies a shallow-draft centerboard boat with a beam approximately half its waterline length, the particulars of the design varying according to where the boats were used. The Cape Cod boats had to operate in the difficult, exposed waters of Nantucket Sound and Buzzards Bay, and tended to be full-bodied, able craft with high bows, transom sterns, and big "barndoor" rudders.

*Although both these catboats, Onaway (**top**) and Oconee, carry racing numbers temporarily affixed to their sails, both would seem to have been equally at home when cruising. Oconee, in particular, has a cabin of large proportions. She is an unusual-looking catboat, with modest freeboard and lines that appear to be very fine, especially toward the stern sections. Her maximum beam looks farther aft than normal. Onaway, with her high bow and barndoor rudder, is a Cape Cod catboat. (Photos by Nathaniel L. Stebbins (Onaway) and Henry Peabody. Courtesy of The Society for the Preservation of New England Antiquities)*

By contrast, typical Barnegat Bay and Great South Bay catboats had markedly less freeboard, a lower bow, and, in their earliest forms, a plumb stem. Generally, they possessed a counter stern and an underhung rudder.

Removable cabins were often fitted, especially to the Jersey cats, and these cabins had colorful canvas curtains that could be rolled up to admit ventilation on humid summer days or rolled down to keep out wind and spray. It was in such a boat, the 20-foot *Coot*, that the outspoken naval architect and yachting critic C.P. Kunhardt cruised singlehanded from Port Morris, New York to Beaufort, North Carolina, and back in the mid-1880s. Kunhardt survived this cruise but admitted he could not have picked a less suitable boat. He advised others *not* to try to duplicate his effort. Catboats like *Coot* had never been intended for such passagemaking.

Whatever their intended purpose or locale, catboats were, with some notable exceptions, designed and built by men with little or no formal training in naval architecture. "The best boats of this type," said the introduction to the *Cat Book*, published by *The Rudder* in 1903, "are those turned out by the rule-of-thumb men. The trained designer generally fails when he tries to produce a catboat." Such failures, it was suggested, resulted from a tampering with the basic elements of the genre—the full ends, great beam, and moderate deadrise. Science or book learning never seems to have helped anybody build a better catboat.

Catboat designer-builders in the classical tradition were whiskery, wrinkled, self-taught men who worked long days, lived to a great age, and relied on the half-models they carved rather than calculations or carefully worked lines plans. The best ones developed an instinct for the necessary proportions and spent a lifetime refining one or two basic designs. There was a certain amount of interchange among them, for the younger ones often apprenticed with those more experienced before packing up their toolboxes and going off to establish their own boatshops.

Manuel Swartz Roberts, who was born on a Martha's Vineyard farm in 1881, was one of those men. He had relatively little schooling and began work as a house carpenter. He built over 200 catboats and became known affectionately to all as the Old Sculpin. One of Manuel's customers even named his boat the *Old Sculpin*. After Roberts died in 1963, his Edgartown shop eventually became an art gallery. It is called the Old Sculpin Gallery.

C.C. Hanley was born in Maine, where he attended grammar school and apprenticed with a manufacturer of piano cases. In 1875 he moved to Cape Cod, where he worked as a blacksmith in Monument Beach and saw his first catboat race. He decided to build a boat of his own and made his first of many models. His catboats became astonishingly successful racers. Yacht designer and M.I.T. professor George Owen called Hanley "a master craftsman and an epoch maker in American yachting." Owen compared him with an M.I.T. graduate who, despite his education, managed to create some very fine catboats of his own. His name was Nathanael Herreshoff.

It was a catboat, in fact, by which Nat Herreshoff demonstrated his genius at an early age. In 1859, when he was not quite 12, Nat, according to his son, L. Francis, "did all the drawing and figuring for the full-size molds" for a 20-foot catboat. This boat was built as a yacht for Nat's blind older brother, John, and was launched in June 1860. Although apparently a brute to steer, *Sprite* earned a lasting reputation for speed, and John, despite his blindness, could sail her to windward as well as

Above: *Catboats gathered at Toms River, New Jersey, circa 1890. (Courtesy Ed Crabbe)*
Right: *Typical of Narragansett Bay catboats is* Laura & Leslie, *built at Saunderstown in 1893 by Martin L. Saunders. The boat was 26 feet 8 inches overall, 12 feet 3 inches in beam, and drew 3 feet 8 inches. An engine was installed in 1906.* Laura & Leslie *was used for fishing and lobstering. (Courtesy John and Laura Saunders)*

anyone. *Sprite*'s 175-mile maiden voyage to New York was completed in 28 hours.

This catboat remained in the Herreshoff family until she was presented as a gift to Henry Ford in 1930. Then she was put on display at the Ford Museum, Ford's personal celebration of American ingenuity and technology. *Sprite*, however, looked out of place amid the industrialist's collection of historic automobiles, all haphazardly arrayed on the largest expanse of teak flooring in the world. The boat was returned to Rhode Island as a loan to the Herreshoff Museum in 1979. She is now the oldest catboat in existence, but she was merely the first of two dozen or more Herreshoff-built catboats of 15 to 28 feet launched between 1860 and 1905.

The Herreshoffs were not the only leading American yacht designers to create catboats as well as larger vessels. A. Cary Smith was apprenticed to Bob Fish in New Jersey in 1855. Smith was the son of an Episcopal minister in New York who, on a Sunday morning, once boasted to a friend: "My father is over in New York preaching heaven and salvation, and I've been over in Gowanus raising Hell and Damnation."

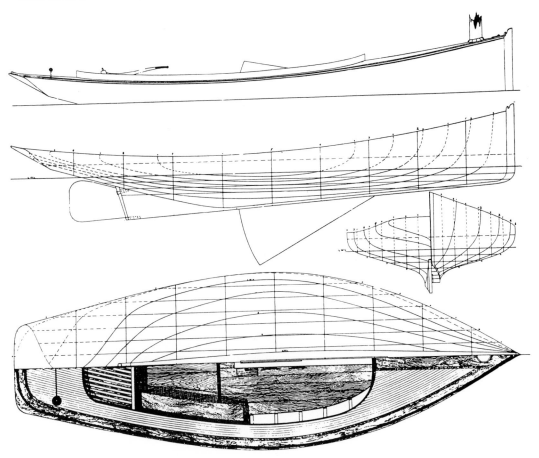

Although she appears to be rather narrow, the Great South Bay catboat Lucile *is similar to New Jersey catboats in her low freeboard. She is a particularly graceful boat, almost dainty in her sections.* Lucile *was built at Patchogue in 1891 by Gilbert Smith.*

Here is Martha, *seven times the winner of the Toms River Challenge Cup, circa 1890.* Martha *is representative of New Jersey catboats of her era, having low sides and an ungainly looking cabin that probably fitted over the coaming and was removable. Despite her size and large sail,* Martha *is tiller steered. (Courtesy Ed Crabbe)*

During a career that ended with his death in 1911, Cary Smith designed everything from catboats to large racing yachts and passenger steamers. He never forgot what the multitalented builder of *Una* taught him about sailing and boat construction. Among catboat racers, Smith's boats were known as the equal of those designed by Nathanael Herreshoff and Charles Mower, indicating they were among the most successful designs of all.

Other catboat builders were less widely known but no less competent. There was William W. Phinney of Monument Beach on Cape Cod, a stocky Methodist who turned out a succession of catboats over his long, productive career. He trained a Maine native named Merton Long who established a boatyard of his own and built many catboats. In Wareham, Massachusetts, Charles Anderson gained a reputation for building graceful catboats of yachtlike finish. There were also "Stormy" John Dexter of Mattapoisett and Henry Lumbert and Walter Carney of Hyannis. In Patchogue, New York, Gilbert Smith created lovely looking boats that enjoyed long-lived success racing in Great South Bay. Smith and his wife often delivered a new boat personally to its owner. G. Frank Carter resided in East Quogue. He lived to be 94 and built over 150 catboats, starting in 1896.

In New Jersey, the shores of Barnegat Bay and the coastal areas around Atlantic City were dotted with professional builders who turned out "rule-of-thumb" catboats by the dozens. Some based their boats on a half-model, others apparently relied entirely on eye and instinct. Among the Jersey builders were the Perrines (J. Howard and Samuel) in Barnegat, John Keith and Ephraim Robinson in Toms River,

With her fantail stern, her long, overhanging boom, and her bowsprit, Mattie *is typical of racing catboats of the early 1890s. The narrow, vertical seams of her cotton sail were created by a process known as* bight seaming, *which involved the folding of tightly woven 28½-inch-wide sailcloth into either 14-inch or nine-inch widths. The resulting narrow panels were strong enough to resist stretch and support the weight of a heavy boom, although they were not as aerodynamically efficient as the crosscut panels pioneered by Nathanael Herreshoff. (Nathaniel L. Stebbins photo. Courtesy of The Society for the Preservation of New England Antiquities)*

and Stanley Van Sant in Atlantic City. The baymen themselves were often capable boatbuilders. Using the abundant clear white cedar and oak from local swamps and forests, they could produce, in a winter's time, a low-sided "Barnegatter" for use in oystering or crabbing. Fast oyster boats often were turned to racing, and bets of several hundred dollars were sometimes wagered on the outcome.

Many of the Jersey-built craft were relatively large, 30 feet and longer, and could carry impressive loads of cargo or passengers. *Olga*, designed by Captain George Cale and his brother Charles for the Atlantic City party trade in 1898, was 43 feet long, and party boats this size and, reputedly, even larger, were not uncommon in

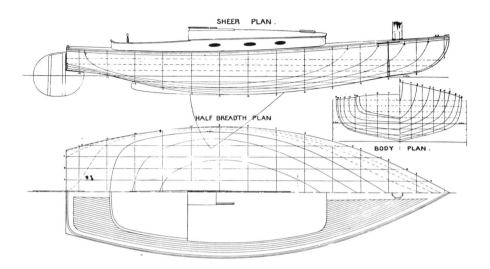

The lines of H. Manley Crosby's Step Lively, *as drawn by naval architect C.G. Davis, show the reverse curve built into the waterline both fore and aft. By this method, the boat's actual waterline could be longer than the load waterline normally used for measurement purposes.* (The Catboat Book, *edited by John M. Leavens)*

New Jersey. There were big catboats in New England, too. For many years, a 38-footer carried freight and passengers from Nantucket town up the harbor to Wauwinet. She had a big black *L* sewn on her sail and was named *Lillian*. Her skipper once counted 105 passengers aboard.

In 1896, Horace Crosby's sons, Manley and Joseph, moved to the Bay Ridge section of Brooklyn, New York, where they lived aboard a grounded-out steamboat and established the Crosby Catboat and Yacht Building Company. The impetus for their move and the new company's treasurer was a wealthy yachtsman named Frank M. Randall who had been racing catboats for some 20 years and wanted to spark interest in the sport in New York. He had indulged himself with the purchase of several boats a year, most built by the Crosbys in Osterville. These boats he endowed with names like *Hit or Miss*, *Win or Lose*, and *Scat*, and he campaigned them successfully.

With a Crosby boatshop close by, Randall commissioned new racing catboats that bore little resemblance to the traditional Cape Cod cats. *Step Lively*, for instance, was 34 feet 9 inches long and, at 11 feet 2 inches beam, narrower than usual. She drew only 1 foot 9 inches with her board up. The lines of "the famous Crosby cat *Step Lively*," as *The Rudder* referred to the boat, show long overhangs with reverse curves at the waterline both fore and aft. Randall promptly entered her in a series of races, most of which she won, and afterward, few people would race against him.

"One of the embarrassing things of being a winner, he found," reported *The Rudder*, "was to go to a race and see all the boats entered drop out or refuse to start when his boat came in sight." Largely for this reason, apparently, catboat racing around New York waned by 1901.

The boats Randall sold usually continued racing. *Scat*, a 26-footer that had been built by Wilton Crosby at Osterville in 1896 and had won 10 races that year, was purchased by Edwin Schoettle, a well-to-do manufacturer of cardboard boxes and the editor of the book *Sailing Craft*, who brought her to Barnegat Bay in 1900. By then, catboat racing in New Jersey was well established, and there was a long tradition of races between baymen and summer visitors. Purses of hundreds of dollars, if not more, were sometimes bet on these competitions. Occasionally the winner took the other man's boat. The Toms River Cup race, which continues to this day, was held for the first time in 1871, when eight catboats of 24 to 26 feet raced from the mouth of Toms River to Forked River and back. Betting on the race was heavy, and armed guards were posted aboard the boats to ward off possible sabotage.

By the time *Scat* arrived in Barnegat Bay, however, the boats competing in the Toms River race and others like it were yachts rather than working craft. Boats like *Scat* and an intensely fast Nat Herreshoff cat named *Merry Thought* essentially ended any hope the older workaday boats had of winning races. The newcomers did so, said Schoettle in *Sailing Craft*, "because of the good hull lines which cheated the waterline length, thus guaranteeing generous handicaps, and because of well cut and designed sails too expensive for the fishermen to duplicate." Schoettle noted that the 32-foot *Merry Thought*, owned by a wealthy Philadelphian named Crozer, cost some $5,000 at a time when "the average builder's price for a 30-foot catboat, completely rigged, was some $1,000 to $1,200." Even those prices were not inexpensive.

In the early 1920s, a new class of 28-foot catboats began racing in Barnegat Bay. The class—called A cats—comprised a half-dozen boats designed by naval architects Charles Mower and Francis Sweisguth. A-cat racing continues to this day, and although the boats require continual maintenance, they generate a high level of affection from their owners and from sailing-oriented bay folk with an eye for tradition. "It made me proud," a Toms River woman told me once, "to have my boy crew aboard the *Mary Ann*."

By the time *Mary Ann* and other A cats were instilling new enthusiasm for catboat racing in Barnegat Bay, the sport in New York and New England had vastly diminished. While racing fleets had once existed in harbors from Boston to the Cape and in Rhode Island, these gradually disappeared, leaving only pockets of activity here or there. Why the decline?

"Better to ask why *not*," said one old-timer.

There have been several suggested causes, among them the "freakish" appearance of some racing catboats, their high cost, or disastrous capsizings and drownings. None of these suffices, however. The yachting press of those days contains few articles about catboat mishaps, and one finds more items about capsizings of other types, including several *schooners*. The cost of a first-class racing catboat certainly was high, but so were the prices of other high-quality racing yachts of similar size. And the oddest-looking catboats were certainly no

It is race day, June 4, 1890, and Moondyne *and* Tartar *beat through smooth water, perhaps in Quincy Bay.* Moondyne *was built in Hyannis by Smalley. Her sprit jib could be winged out when running before the wind.* Tartar *is unusual in her lapstrake construction. She has the plum stem and rakish lines of a sandbagger and must surely have raced in a different class than* Moondyne. *(Nathaniel L. Stebbins photo. Courtesy of The Society for the Preservation of New England Antiquities)*

more peculiar than some of the newly developed keep sloops or the skinny, deep-draft "plank on edge cutters."

The catboat grew as the sport of sailing grew, and, inevitably, it faced competition from more modern types. During the late 19th and early 20th centuries, yacht club debates and magazine columns considered the advantages of keel boats versus centerboarders and of cutter versus sloop or cat rigs. Cutter enthusiasts were so vociferous they earned the nickname "cutter cranks," and these sailors with their affection for deep keels were certainly among the detractors of centerboard boats, whether rigged as sloops or catboats. Given such competition and the changing times, there is little wonder that the catboat fell gradually behind the times. What really finished it as a racing yacht, however, was World War I.

"After that," said C. Willis Garey, "it just never got going again. Somehow the boats got sold off to different places and the people weren't the same. What finished us was the Kaiser."

The racing of those big catboats required strength and skill, for 25-footers regularly set 1,000 square feet of sail or more. Here is how Winfield Thompson, a longtime catboat sailor and regular contributor to *The Rudder*, described the tacking of a racing catboat built by C.C. Hanley. A 250-pound man handled the mainsheet. "Quickly the sheet came in, and quickly also over the lee rail came a couple of barrels or so of water. When a boat of 12-foot breadth dips up the brine thus freely under four reefs, you may believe there is a snap and weight to the breeze. The Commodore was sailing her as nearly on edge as he had ever done."

Five or six men, including the skipper, normally constituted the crew of a boat like this. One was assigned to handle the mainsheet, which often belayed to a big cleat on the cockpit sole at the cabin. Usually, if a strong wind was blowing, a second hand was placed on the sheet. Another crewman was assigned duty as centerboard tender. Another might see to the boat's navigation, while the remainder would fill in as necessary and tend backstays, if required, or the jib or spinnaker if those were permitted by class rules.

Among the last bastions of New England catboat racing was the Massachusetts Bay Catboat Association. Said Winfield Thompson of its membership in 1908: "The lust of variety is not one of their yachting sins. They know the worth of a good thing and hold fast to it .... They love the type of boat they represent. Their patron saints are the Crosbys of Osterville and C.C. Hanley, the best builders of catboats. They know every cat of note on the Atlantic coast, and can tell the work of different builders at a distant glance." Even this enthusiasm, however, did not survive the Great War. The old racing catboats were sold off and scattered as the art and science of yacht racing continued to evolve and times began to change in dramatic ways.

"Those were the days," Manuel Swartz Roberts said once of the less hurried years when catboats were common. "They were happy days, but we didn't know it at the time."

It was out of a catboat race held at Saybrook, Connecticut, in 1962 that the present-day Catboat Association grew. Its founders intended to sponsor a series of modest races for cruising catboats and provide a common ground for all those interested in the boats' history. Some 60 people had joined by the time the Association held its first annual winter meeting at Mystic Seaport in the winter of 1963. The group grew slowly, but a decade later, there were some 300 members. Then something surprising happened; the membership began to swell like a sail filling in a fresh breeze. The roster billowed upward to 500, 800, and, at last count, over 1,200.

"It is a constant source of amazement and gratification," said John Leavens of the Association's growth. Beginning when the group was formed, Leavens remained its prime mover for years, relinquishing his command only after an illness in the late 1970s. Born in Newark, New Jersey, in 1907, Leavens spent summers at his family's home in Brielle. He recalls being allowed to raise the sail on a rental catboat at the boatyard run there by S. Bartley Pearce. "He'd let me hoist

With a nattily dressed party aboard, Varona *sails on a broad reach, probably along Boston's South Shore. (Nathaniel L. Stebbins photo. Courtesy of The Society for the Preservation of New England Antiquities)*

the sail to dry after it rained. I'd raise the sail and let the boat drift back to the end of its painter." He learned to sail in an old sneakbox and haunted the Jersey boatyards, including Johnson Brothers. "I used to like to see the catboats there," he said. "You could hire them for a party sail."

Leavens never lost his boyhood fascination with catboats. He bought a Crosby-built catboat and ceaselessly pursued every scrap of information about catboats of all sorts, adding a collection of old half-models to an impressive assemblage of duck decoys. When Howard Chapelle sought some catboat half-models to add to the Smithsonian's collection, he got the carvings from John Leavens. The models he sent had been made by Manuel Swartz Roberts.

"They sent Manuel a letter," he remembered, "and in their annual report, they listed Manuel and me as donors. I told Manuel, 'Well, Manuel, you're famous *now*. You've got a model in the Smithsonian Institution!'"

Together with his wife Pinkie, Leavens has, with the assistance of some key Catboat Association members, managed to guide the organization successfully without ever holding an election or establishing bylaws. In 1963, he began publishing the Association's *Bulletin*, including stories about the old-time builders John studied. When possible, he interviewed those who had built catboats, those who had once raced, and those who had used a catboat for work. It is the latter breed of catboater, now all but extinct, that possesses an inherent fascination for today's enthusiasts.

Winter, 1916, and part of Nantucket's 60-boat scallop fleet lies iced in at Old North Wharf. A culling board is mounted on the coaming of the nearest catboat. (Courtesy Charles F. Sayle, Sr.)

"When you stop to think that people's livelihoods and *lives* once depended on these catboats," said one Catboat Association member, "why that really gets you wondering *how* they did it."

Crewed by a man and a boy, the fishing cats worked year-round, dredging scallops and pursuing mackerel, cod, bluefish, and, with bow pulpits from which to toss a harpoon, swordfish. Joseph Chase Allen, bard of Martha's Vineyard, grew up with these old-time catboatmen and remembered them when he addressed The Catboat Association in 1967. "They were stiff-necked, self-sufficient and they detested anyone who was inquisitive . . . . They taught me how to splice a line and how to tie most of the working knots when my fingers were so small they had to use a piece of clothesline. I couldn't handle anything heavier. They taught me the sails of a square-rigged ship before I could even read."

The exploits of such men have long since passed into legend. They weathered storms, survived leaks, fires, and cold, and viewed all these hazards as an acceptable part of a fisherman's life. Year after year, their catboats carried them forth from harbor and brought the great majority of them safely home again. "They smelled their way through fog and snowstorms," said Allen. Few bothered with compasses. "The catboat men just headed in the general direction of North America and they usually fetched up all right. I don't know how they did it because they took short cuts along the shore and across such places as Devils Bridge where some of the rocks stand out of water and some are just awash when the tide comes in."

During the first years of the 1900s, fishermen began equipping their catboats with inboard engines—the single-cylinder Lathrops, Knoxes, and Palmers they referred to as "putt-putts" or "bait mills." Rigs began to shrink and, in some instances, were removed altogether as more powerful and reliable marine engines were developed. Thus began the decline of the catboat as a working craft and party

By the early 1920s, some large catboats had been given pilot houses and deeper holds, and were used as draggers and for quahogging. The boats are moored at Steamboat Wharf, Nantucket. (Courtesy Charles F. Sayle, Sr.)

fishing boat. The working fleets had already diminished in size by 1910, but some catboats remained in use well into the 1930s. Oscar Pease, who has been involved with catboats all his life on Martha's Vineyard, recalls that not until the destructive hurricane of 1938 did the island's catboats finally succumb altogether.

Unlike some of the racing catboats, the workboats never developed to bizarre extremes. They retained the wholesome, straightforward qualities proved over many decades, and it was this that attracted those yachtsmen unmoved by the latest thinking in design. Catboat sailors tend to be people who value simplicity of rig and traditional looks more than the latest yachts or sailing gadgets. They have

After a successful day of quahog dredging, the catboat Idlewild *is unloaded at Old North Wharf, Nantucket. Boats like this towed 15- to 18-inch dredges from a tackle rigged on the gaff. (Courtesy Charles F. Sayle, Sr.)*

less interest in the exploits of modern fin-keel ocean racers than in the subtle tricks and techniques used by the independent old-time fishermen or by yachtsmen of an earlier era. That self-sufficient breed was most notably represented by a bespectacled Harvard man named Henry Plummer.

In 1912, Plummer made a cruise from New Bedford to Miami and back in a 24-foot catboat called *Mascot*. With him were his son and a cat. Plummer kept a log of this eight-month, eight-day odyssey—which included a stranding on Carolina's outer banks thanks to an inaccurate chart—and eventually wrote a book about the experience. He titled it, *The Boy, Me and the Cat*, and it has become a kind of small classic of cruising literature, a modest monument to enthusiasm, endurance, and the sheer indomitability of the devoted small-boat sailor.

Plummer took a number of photographs during his trip. One of them shows *Mascot* and her inboard-powered launch anchored off the entrance to the Delaware and Raritan Canal in New Brunswick, New Jersey. In the background, one can see an arched bridge. The bridge is still there; *Mascot* and the world to which she belonged have disappeared.

What remains of them is an enduring nostalgia for Plummer's book and for boats like *Mascot*. She sank in a refueling accident near Friendship, Maine, in 1947 but was eventually hauled out and used by a local lobsterman to store his traps.

Finally the hulk was burned. It was the peculiar reverence that catboat enthusiasts exhibit for the little vessels that prompted John Saunders—whose ancestors in Rhode Island began building catboats over 100 years ago—to look for any surviving bits of *Mascot*. He and his wife, Laura, who live in Friendship, found the old catboat's big centerboard.

"It was still there in the grass," Laura Saunders told me. "We persuaded the owners of the property to let us have it and managed to put it on top of our Subaru."

The board is the same one that was in *Mascot* for Plummer's voyage to Florida, 70 years ago. Now the Saunderses own it. They keep it, a decaying but evocative shrine, in a field behind their house.

2

Oscar

IT HAD NOT BEEN what he called a good season. It was only the second week of November, the second week of the season, but down on Cape Poge, five miles from Edgartown, there were few places where a man would find scallops he could call "good stock."

"There were 35 boats down there to Cape Poge on the first day, down to where the good stock is, and they cleaned 'em out in one day. So they moved out to another place and caught smaller stock. So it went. Just like that. It seems this year, down there where there normally would be a good-quality scallop, it just isn't there."

Oscar Pease talked as we walked across the perfectly manicured expanse of grass that is his backyard. It was just about 5:45 A.M. on November 17, and our insulated seaboots rustled softly on the lawn. We carried oilskins and sweaters and a Thermos full of cold, fresh water. Gray clouds moved across the dark sky, and a northwest breeze rattled softly in the bare trees.

"Of course," Oscar said, "there are areas down there, down off Cape Poge, that need a great amount of wind to move some of the dirt off the bottom so more scallops will show up."

We piled our gear into the back seat of Oscar's blue Dodge Omni and hooked up his trailer. The wooden trailer bed was mounted on leaf springs salvaged from a Ford Model T. The wire wheels and axle had come from a Model A. The trailer was 46 years old, but it looked brand-new. Into its bed, Oscar lifted a number of wire

27

bushel baskets and a bright red five-gallon gas can. Then we got into the car and drove off slowly through the quiet streets of Edgartown. We passed picket fences, a house with a neatly curtained oval window in its door, and tidy frame houses. We passed American Legion Post 186, where Oscar serves as adjutant. There, the night before, we had bowed our heads while Bob Convery, the post chaplain, said a prayer for America. Only five legionnaires were there, together with their wives since it was ladies' night, but Oscar conducted the meeting as officially and efficiently as if a battalion had showed up.

A few blocks from Post 186, we turned down a driveway paved with scallop shells. Oscar backed the trailer down to the end of the driveway where a long wooden pier ran out into the harbor. While I unloaded the trailer, Oscar launched his eight-foot flat-bottomed skiff by rolling it over the sand beach on a roller made of laths, until the boat floated gently in the gray water. He had built the skiff in 1939, but it looked brand-new. It took him only a few minutes to row silently out to where *Vanity*, his catboat, lay moored. He climbed aboard and tied the skiff off carefully. Then, there was a brief puff of white exhaust smoke and Oscar was soon on his way in. He pulled alongside the dock slowly, taking a mooring line to a wooden cleat on the stern. Then he shut off the engine while I handed down the wire baskets and the gas can that he promptly emptied into a tank on the boat's port side. He emptied it carefully and did not spill a drop.

"This can," he said when he had finished, "is galvanized inside and out. This can is 50 years old." He wiped it off and stowed it.

I climbed down into the boat as Oscar flicked a toggle switch and brought the engine instantly to life. "Quick as a tick" is what he says of engines that start promptly or boats that come about easily. He cast off the mooring line and moved the gear lever forward, and the boat backed away. He bent over the tiller, looking backward and steering with two hands until there was room enough to swing around and point the bow toward the harbor mouth. Then he shifted into forward and tapped the throttle with his foot. We slipped along through the placid water, past the squat lighthouse on Starbuck Neck and past a beach where rotting seaweed gave off a sulfurous stench that was borne down to us on the breeze.

From a few scattered moorings, other boats were heading out. We came up past Chappaquiddick, where Oscar's grandfather was born in 1824 and grew to become a whaling skipper.

"That was *before* they had catboats," said Oscar.

We passed by the low black hull of the Chappaquiddick ferryboat. One July day in 1937, when the ferry was carrying a laundry truck to the island, a seaplane swooped down to land in the harbor, and its rudder jammed. The pilot did his best to turn the airplane to the right but the machine circled left instead. A wing and a pontoon struck the ferry and the plane dove right down into the water. The first vessel to reach the struggling survivors was a catboat owned by Walter Brown. He plucked two passengers from the wreckage, and the Coast Guard saved the rest.

As we emerged from Edgartown Harbor, we met the swell raised up by the wind, low gray-green seas rolling in just off the bow. Oscar tapped the throttle again and *Vanity* picked up speed, leaping into the seas at eight knots and, now and then, casting up some spray.

Rigged for scalloping, Vanity *shows the frame from which the drags are set, an enclosed steering position for bad weather, and the midships culling board. (Stan Grayson photo)*

"I don't do this much for business nowadays," Oscar said. "Mostly I just go because I like to and to get something to eat."

The sharp bow split a wave and spray spattered against our yellow oilskins with a sound like that of small pebbles hitting glass. The other boats, faster, were now ahead of us—outboard-powered skiffs, a dory or two, small workboats of many types, and a lobster boat. We plodded along after them, the only catboat in the fleet. Each November for half a century, missing only the years when Oscar was off-island for World War II, *Vanity* has gone scalloping. Of the many hundreds of catboats that once worked the waters between Cape Cod and New Jersey, only *Vanity* remains. She is all that is left of the great fleets. She is the last working Cape Cod catboat in America.

In 1912, when Oscar Pease was born, there were dozens of catboats on Martha's Vineyard and many more on Nantucket and in Cape Cod's shallow harbors. That same year, Oscar's father bought a 23-foot catboat that had been built by the Crosbys in Osterville in 1900. With this boat, Thomas Pease went scalloping during the winter months. In the spring, he hauled the boat and painted it. Then he launched it again and sailed it in the summer party trade.

"It was the summer people," said Oscar. "They'd want to go out in a boat and they'd hire different captains to take them around. At 10 or 11 in the morning, they'd be taken over to the beach club, now known as the Chappaquiddick Beach Club, for a swim. Then they'd come back by one and have their lunch and then have the captain take them for a sail, or perhaps they would go fishing somewhere or for a picnic on a beach."

Gentle summer days like that were the rule then on the Vineyard, and they followed, one upon the other, in a sun-washed parade of tranquillity, until the Great War came along and the routine changed forever. "After that," said Oscar, "there were cars. People didn't have so much use for boats. They could *drive* to a beach."

For Thomas Pease, the change was no particular loss. "He got fed up," said Oscar, "fed up with the idea of taking people for hire and being their lackey so to speak."

Thomas Pease wanted to be his own boss. He wanted to be free, he sometimes said, "to go to work at three A.M. if I please." He gave up sailing summer people to Chappaquiddick and went after quahogs, some as big as baseballs, that lay upon the harbor bottom. He sailed his boat out to a likely quahog bed and anchored. Then, with a 24-foot-long hard pine pole and a basket rake, he raked the bottom, drawing up a rich harvest. Once, just to prove the worth of his self-employment, he really did go quahogging at three A.M. He worked thus with his Crosby catboat for some five years until the vessel needed repairs. Then he went to New Bedford and bought a 17-footer.

This boat, of undetermined origin, must have been built as a fishing boat, for a fish well that was nearly half the size of her cockpit had been installed. At the time he bought the boat, this well was plugged up, and Thomas Pease took the boat to the best-known catboat builder on the Vineyard to have the well restored. Manuel Swartz Roberts did the job, and Pease returned to his quahogging, going out at five o'clock each morning and returning to Edgartown by 9:30 to sell his catch. Then he went back out again, fishing for scup. Before noon, he would be back, with 200 pounds of fish swimming in the well Manuel had made for him.

"People would come and look at the fish and ask where he got 'em and Father would say, 'yup, nope, yup, nope.' He didn't give 'em much information."

The scup weighed about 2½ pounds each and were caught on a handline trailed over the side of the catboat. When he hauled the fish aboard, Thomas Pease tossed them in his well where they would thrash and bang until they learned there was to be no escape. "That," said Oscar, "would sort of supple 'em down. That and when a couple got in there. That would supple them down, too. That was good because the other fish in the water would knock off biting until everything was quiet and there wasn't that sound anymore."

After the trapped scup suppled down, those still in the water would sneak out of their hiding places in the seaweed and go for the bait made up of salted scallop guts. The line Thomas Pease tossed to the scup was light and lightly weighted so that it made no splash as it hit the water. The line would settle gradually with its irresistible promise and the fish would bite again.

"I'm telling you," said Oscar, who began to fish with his father at age 4, "it was great fun to get two of those big scup on a light line like that."

By the time Oscar was 16, his father decided it was time to buy a new, larger catboat. "He figured I'd be going fishing with him so he figured he should have a bigger boat where the two of us could go," is how Oscar remembers the decision.

There was never any question about who would build the boat. One day in 1928, Thomas Pease walked down to Manuel Swartz Roberts's cedar-shingled boatshop. "Well, Manuel," he said, "I've got a thousand dollars of interest money and I think I'd like you to build me a 20-foot boat. I want a centerboard, a fish well, a six horsepower Lathrop engine, and will you do it?"

Manuel, a slender man who wore baggy pants and shirts buttoned to the collar, listened to the fisherman. "Well," he said, "I'll build you the boat as you state for a thousand dollars."

By the time Thomas Pease ordered his new catboat, Manuel Swartz Roberts had probably built some 140 examples of the type. His shop was famous even then, and Joseph Chase Allen once described it like this in the *Vineyard Gazette*: "Manuel's was a place where the deep-sea colloquial was commonplace. Strangers sometimes asked what, exactly, the assembly was talking about. For someone was forereaching on someone else, someone else had been hove down with bilge trouble and Manuel was laying out a great circle course to follow with his band saw."

Manuel Swartz, for such is the way he was commonly referred to, began his working life at age 17, learning the rudiments of woodworking by helping to build houses. He moved about the Vineyard on various construction projects, from

Katama to West Tisbury and then to Vineyard Haven, where he nearly severed a finger with a saw. While recovering, he worked on a house owned by G.W. Eldridge, creator of the *Eldridge Tide and Pilot Book*. By then, Manuel had more or less decided he was more interested in the idea of building boats than the reality of building houses.

"I worked on a house for Colonel Wise," Manuel told Catboat Association founder John Leavens. "The foreman put me on circular work. That is anything that has to do with rounds and circles. 'You want to be a boatbuilder,' says he, 'so damn it, you do circular work.'"

Not long afterward, Manuel concluded that while doing his circular work on houses, he always got the coldest corner in winter and the warmest one in summer. When this perception clarified itself, he walked into the West Tisbury boatshop of William King and asked King this question: "Do you think you can teach me to put two pieces of wood together so they will be watertight?" The warmth of the boatbuilder's woodstove struck Manuel full in the face.

Two years after he began his apprenticeship, Manuel found himself suddenly on his own when King retired. "Manuel," said the boatbuilder, "I've been watching you for a long time. You go right ahead. You'll do all right."

Manuel went home to his parents' farm near Katama. There, using six by eight-inch timbers salvaged from a wrecked coasting schooner, he erected the framework for his first boatshop and built his first boat. Like nearly every boat then being turned out at Edgartown, it was a catboat, a 17-footer whose owner named it *Constitution* after one of the most famous racing yachts of that era. A second boat, an 18-footer named *Sophie*, followed.

Like most catboat builders, Manuel Swartz had no formal training in naval architecture. He had seen how William King planned a boat on a scale of one inch to one foot, drawing the boat's lines on paper ruled out with one-inch squares. Manuel drew his own lines on the paper, using French curves. He said he worked from experience and from what he could observe in other boats.

"I just worked out the design as I went along," he liked to say.

By the time he had worked out his second boat, he had decided to move to Edgartown, where he built about a dozen more catboats before moving into an old cedar-shingled sail loft on Dock Street in 1905. This particular building was reinforced by iron tie-rods, so it had remained standing despite the hurricanes that occasionally swept the island, blowing other sail lofts away. Manuel built boats on the ground floor of his shop; upstairs, he installed his band saw and milling machine.

At the time *Vanity*'s keel was laid, Manuel had a young helper from Vineyard Haven named Erford Burt. He was a natural woodworker, an essential talent for anyone who hoped to get along with the boatbuilder. It took Manuel about four months to complete a catboat. Burt's presence did not slow him down.

"Manuel wouldn't explain to anybody, 'do this, do that,'" said Oscar. "If you were sharp enough, while you worked there, you could pick this up on your own and it was so much the better for you."

Manuel Swartz Roberts was a talkative man, but he did *not* talk about his work.

As soon as Manuel found out that Erford Burt could caulk a seam and drill the long holes necessary for doweling together rudders and centerboards, he turned over this work to his assistant.

"That was my job," Burt remembered. "I did the drilling and the caulking." Burt did not seem to resent the special tasks he was assigned. Years later, when talking about the building of catboats, he said: "There's a lot of know-how goes into building a catboat and it takes a lifetime of experience to get to know all the tricks of the trade. Back in the old days, you could pick them up by working with a master as I did working for Manuel Swartz Roberts . . . . "

Construction of *Vanity* was begun in the winter of 1928. In Chilmark, Thomas Pease had seen another 20-footer built by Manuel, and wanted a duplicate. The full-bowed cat in Chilmark was 12 years old, but Manuel had saved all the molds, or so he thought. He had stacked them up here and there in corners of his boatshop, nailed them to walls, or stowed them outside. From diverse places, he gathered the molds together, set them up, and went to work. The work went smoothly, too. It was not until the hull was completed that Thomas Pease took a critical look at it and realized something was wrong.

"Dammit, Manuel," he said, "this boat don't look like that one in Chilmark. This is like a flat-iron [skiff] at the front, quite sharp forward, no bulge to the bow. What happened here, Manuel?"

The boatbuilder stared critically at his handiwork. He thought for a while. He scratched his head and peered at the now-offensive bow. "Now that I think of it," he said, shaking his head, "I believe I added to the form originally to fill her out forward on deck more, but the damn pieces must have got knocked off the molds."

Thomas Pease listened with disbelief. He had paid a thousand dollars for a boat that had the wrong shape. "That bow," said Oscar, "was the consequence of being the difference of the two boats. Oh, Father was unhappy about it."

With her sharp bow, *Vanity* immediately proved herself a comparatively wet boat. But she was also comparatively fast, the fastest boat in Edgartown, according to Oscar. Her speed was achieved despite her weight, for Manuel always put a lot of wood into his boats. Pease's new boat, which carried no rig, was powered by a two-cycle, single-cylinder, six horsepower Lathrop purchased from Manuel, who was the island's Lathrop dealer. The engine was equipped with a low-tension make-and-break ignition system, the sort that helped give such machines their legendary reliability. It turned a big 18 by 24-inch propeller that gave ample thrust whether going forward or backward.

Despite her overly sharp bow, Thomas Pease's new boat was a handsome one, with gracefully curved coamings, steady sheer, and a single oval portlight on each side of her short cabin. "Father saw she was good-looking," said Oscar, "and he knew Manuel had built some homely damn boats. This one here was just a mistake."

Thomas Pease and his wife sat down with a dictionary and looked up the word *vanity*. It was defined, in part, as being an "idle show." Pease decided his boat might be showy but that she would never be idle. He liked the irony in this and promptly christened her *Vanity*. A pious waterfront character besieged Pease with the accusation, "Do you know what your boat's name *means*?"

Pease just smiled.

Thomas Pease had begun his life as a fisherman when he was still a boy. At that time, most Vineyard fishermen worked seven days a week. They awoke at about three in the morning and did their best to make it out to the fishing grounds by nine. Mostly, they did not get home again until nine or 10 at night, by which time they were ready to eat and go to sleep so they could get up once again at three.

"Things only got operative with the wife," said Oscar of those times, "in harder weather." By the time Thomas Pease began fishing on his own, most boats were equipped with gas engines. The engines' promise was immediately recognized by men who promptly decided they had rowed and sailed to work for too long. The engines meant a shorter day, a shorter week, and more chance to "get operative" with the wife on fair days as well as foul. If they were primarily shellfishing, the men worked a six-day week. If they sought mackerel or bluefish or another species that was in the area on a seasonal basis, they worked every day they could.

During the spring, some of the Vineyard fleet sailed to Block Island to intercept the mackerel run on its way up the coast. Then the usual crew of one man and one boy would be supplemented with an additional fisherman or two, depending on the boat's size. Sometimes a catboat would tow a 16-foot dory loaded with additional gear and nets. The nets were set by anchors or rigged with floats, the boat being made fast to the net's downwind end. Then the nets and the catboats would drift through the water and, at night, twinkling lanterns atop six-foot bamboo poles would attract the fish. Larger catboats regularly went after swordfish, taking along a hold full of ice to keep their catch fresh. Occasionally, the largest catboats ventured to Georges Bank, a three-day sail, in search of fish.

"That would seem to me to be pretty hairy," said Oscar, "but then again, that was their livelihood. It was pretty risky, a hard way to live."

For a decade after *Vanity* was launched, Thomas Pease used her daily to make a living. He supplemented his income by working with Manuel, helping with the hauling and storage of boats at the Chappaquiddick yard the builder owned. Oscar worked there, too. They launched boats on rollers for a time until Manuel built a proper railway. *Vanity* was used as a towboat in those days, and Oscar learned all about boats of all types and how to rig them.

The great unnamed hurricane of 1938 destroyed this boatyard of Manuel's, and fish catches seemed to diminish thereafter, too. When that happened, Thomas Pease decided it was time to install a rig in his boat and supplement his income by once again taking summer visitors out sailing. The boat had been built with a centerboard to improve her maneuverability under power. Now she needed spars and a sail. The mast was built from a spruce log washed off the deck of a coasting schooner. Erford Burt made it. He found the log on a beach and towed it home behind his Essex coupe.

Vanity's sail plan was copied from a Crosby boat called *Four Aces.* "I tell you," said Oscar, "there weren't many boats around here that could touch her [*Four Aces*] under sail. She was a 23-foot boat. The mast was 29 feet and the boom was the same length as the mast. The gaff, when put against the mast, came aft to the boom crutch. That was the formula. Then you hoisted the peak up to where it looked good and took your measurement down for the sail leech."

Manuel had built extra strength into *Vanity*'s bow just so the boat would be easily adaptable to a mast. His main concern was to cut the oak mast step until it was perfectly level. The first time the mast was lowered into the boat, it had a decided rake aft, "piratical" as Oscar remembers it.

"Manuel," said Oscar, "did a few figures, something mathematical. He did something like measure from the deck down to the keel and made marks thinking about how much the mast would tip forward if he cut down so much to the keel step."

Manuel did his few figures quickly, blithely cut the mast step down by some 2½ inches, lowered the mast back in, and wedged it. It stood perfectly straight. Fittings and blocks were ordered from catalogs and a sail was ordered from a New Bedford loft. Thomas Pease fashioned the gaff and boom himself, making the gaff eight-sided to save weight aloft.

By the summer of 1939, *Vanity* was sailing for the first time, and the Peases were pleased with her qualities. This was something of a surprise to them, especially to Oscar, who had worked summers as skipper of a Crosby catboat owned by a summer resident. Manuel's boats were not thought to possess the same sailing qualities as a Crosby, perhaps because they were invariably overbuilt. Thomas Pease claimed the Crosby boats were built lighter and more flexibly than Manuel's.

"Why," he'd say, "if you wanted to close the cabin doors on a Crosby boat while it was sailing, you might not be able to. The boat would be twisted in such a way that they wouldn't fit."

Manuel never did much sailing. He contented himself with a 17-foot catboatlike hull in which he fitted a one-lunger engine and a steering station protected by a wheelhouse up forward. "Manuel's boating," said Oscar, "was *workboating*."

In the summer of 1982, I had the opportunity briefly to sail aboard *Vanity*, for Oscar had sailed her over to Osterville for the annual Catboat Association get-together at Townsend Hornor's house. That was the first time I had seen the boat afloat, instead of under the tree in Oscar's backyard where *Vanity* is stored from mid-December through spring. She is a graceful-looking boat. Perhaps the most notable thing about her, and a key to her working origin, is her comparatively long cockpit. It's a workspace, a place in which a man can walk back and forth easily, a place to make a living.

By contrast, the cabin is small. There are two rather narrow berths there, and some space in the forepeak that Oscar uses to stow neatly coiled lines and other gear. Had Manuel built *Vanity* as a cruising boat, the cabin would extend back some five additional feet. The cabin, which is entered through a companionway on the starboard side, remains a snug refuge in bad weather. It is comfortable enough for occasional nights aboard, too, even for a large-boned man like Oscar. He was, in fact, spending that summer weekend aboard, lamenting not the fact that the cabin was small but that, although his wife, Nellie, had packed him lunches full of tasty sandwiches and the baked goods for which she is justly renowned, he had forgotten to bring a blanket.

Vanity was painted white, mauve, and dark green. There was not a hint of buff, the traditional color for catboat decks and cabintops, even though Manuel had originally used buff. Thomas Pease, however, happened to get a bargain on gray paint from Sears, Roebuck, and for years *Vanity* has been predominantly "dove gray" with a white hull and coamings. To this basic color scheme Oscar has added

Catboat Association rendezvous, Oscar at the wheel. (Stan Grayson photo)

the mauve cabintop and seats and the dark green cockpit sole. At first glance, *Vanity* looks like a waterborne version of one of Oak Bluffs' brightly painted Victorian cottages. According to Oscar, the color scheme is "similar to the old Crosby colors."

Oscar himself was brightly dressed in a pair of red pants, a blue shirt, and blue sneakers. In the time before we raised sail to join the traditional parade of boats around Osterville Grand Island, he described the features of the boat, beginning with the focal point, the engine. *Vanity* is now powered by a 45 horsepower, four-cylinder Lathrop. This engine was installed in 1938 when the original two-cycle Lathrop finally wore out. Like most of the fishermen on Martha's Vineyard, Oscar refers to one-lungers as "putt-putts."

"The fact that my father had a putt-putt as late as 1938," he said, "indicates how successful the early make-and-break engine really was."

He remembers the one-lunger for its vast torque and the weight of its big red flywheel. "Sometimes," he said, "it seemed like it took a day's work just starting those things, even though they had a compression release." The six-horsepower's power is nowhere better illustrated than by the fact that the 45 horsepower machine that replaces it turns a far smaller—16 by 10 versus 18 by 24—propeller, albeit at higher speed.

The block forward makes it easy to handle the ground tackle from Vanity's *cockpit. (Stan Grayson photo)*

The engine now in *Vanity* is, in fact, the second LH4. It is nestled beneath the cockpit sole like some gray-painted centerpiece. Upon this machine Oscar has lavished uncounted hours of creative thought. He devised each accessory, each water valve and hose to be *just so*, modifying components as necessary to fit his overall scheme. It is one of those engines one often hears about but seldom sees, an engine you could *eat* off. Dentistlike, Oscar uses a little mirror to reveal the bottom of the intake manifold when he touches things up with his glossy gray enamel.

Vanity is as well cared for as her engine or, for that matter, Oscar's ancient red gas can. In 1981, he put 13 new frames in her starboard side, cutting down two-inch oak timbers to 1½-inch thickness because he could not purchase wood in the size he wanted. The boat's simple finish is kept up, too, and when he goes scalloping Oscar covers up his painted coamings with fitted wooden caps. He indicated that such meticulousness just came naturally to anybody from Edgartown but that "over to Gay Head, they don't take much care of boats."

When it was time to go sailing, Oscar tied off his skiff to the anchor line. Then he pressed the starter, and sure enough, the Lathrop fired right up, quick as a tick. We powered our way slowly through the drawbridge connecting the mainland with Osterville Grand Island, and, in the constricted channel, Oscar handed over the wheel and prepared to raise sail. He moved slowly, casting off the sail gaskets and taking up on the topping lift, and then he began smoothly to haul on the throat and peak halyards.

There was a light following breeze, and when we switched off the engine, *Vanity*

Jogging along near Osterville. (Stan Grayson photo)

moved slowly through the water. Her rig, at 250 square feet, is small for a catboat of her size and 4,200-pound displacement, about the same size as that of a lighter, fiberglass, 18-footer. Had *Vanity* originally been built without an engine, her sail area might have been twice what it is. Being a man who takes things in stride, not given to hurrying, Oscar seems never to have contemplated increasing the sail area of his boat. Since he singlehands so much of the time, the rig has proved perfect. His wisdom in this was evident shortly after we had raised the sail, when the breeze freshened and headed us. Then I was glad of the big oak quarter cleats around which the mainsheet could be wound.

Vanity proved herself nimble and well balanced, possessed of only modest weather helm. Since we were among more than 20 other catboats, it was easy to compare *Vanity*'s speed and pointing ability, and she compared favorably with other wooden catboats her size, even those with larger sails. Like most wooden catboats, *Vanity* doesn't want to be pinched too much, and by easing the sheet just a bit and bearing off slightly, one can improve her progress to windward radically.

Oscar, of course, knows all this. He seems as much a part of *Vanity* as her keel. He likes to sit right aft on one of the comfortable seats, peering up now and then at the sail, making minor trim changes as necessary. He gets the best from *Vanity* by instinct and still takes obvious delight in her performance, even after 43 years at her brightly varnished wheel.

We reached the scalloping grounds in Cape Poge Pond at precisely seven A.M. and could not help noticing that, although it is lawful to fish only from seven until four, at least one boat had begun early. *Vanity* was rigged to pull four drags, two from each side of a galvanized framework that Oscar has designed. Quickly, Oscar dropped the port drags overboard, followed soon afterward by those to starboard. The lines ran out over the unfinished wooden pieces that protect the coamings, then down into the water. In the spring, Oscar removes the cover pieces, fills the nail holes with putty, and paints the caprail so that it looks brand-new.

Pulling the drags along the bottom, which Oscar judged to be eight feet beneath us, made little difference to *Vanity*. The boat plodded dutifully ahead, obedient as some well-trained workhorse, while Oscar steered with the tiller between his legs. He replaces the wheel with a tiller at scalloping time for just this reason. Each fall, too, he replaces *Vanity*'s regular hatch cover with a built-up sort of wheelhouse-cum-hatch. In hard weather, he can stand below, peering out through the wheelhouse windows while steering the boat with tiller lines.

We had towed the drags for some 10 minutes when Oscar judged it was time to haul them in and see what we had caught. Years earlier, he had hauled the dredges in hand over hand, just as some of the fishermen in the dories were doing. But now, Oscar hauls mechanically. He takes a turn of line around a winch head driven by belt and pulley off the engine, and the drag is quickly, effortlessly hauled home. The first one came up over the side dripping water and weeds. Oscar lowered it onto the culling board that runs right across *Vanity*. He upended the contents of the drag and we began tossing grass and the larger stones back overboard.

The first scallops showed up beneath the grass, and Oscar tossed them into a wire basket about half the size of the bushel baskets we had brought aboard. I started to find more scallops, hidden in the grass, and tossed them into the basket, too. We seemed to have quite a haul of fine scallops in this first batch, plump fan-shaped shellfish colored soft brown and beige. We tossed one after another into the basket. Out of the water, the scallops started opening and closing their shells. They made a noise like that of plastic poker chips clicking together, and somehow evoked a basketfull of unhappy scallop muppets.

It took less than four minutes to cull through the contents of the first drag. Immediately, Oscar tossed it back and brought aboard the second drag. We culled through it. Then came the third drag and the fourth. Then Oscar turned the boat 180 degrees and we began to haul the drags back in the opposite direction. There seemed to be many scallops in the drags and the work did not appear too difficult. Sometimes, I had trouble telling if a scallop was good, whether or not the shell was empty or, maybe, just full of gritty mud.

"You take 'em and tap their hinge on the cullin' board," advised Oscar, "and if they're bad, they'll fall open. Sometimes, you can tell by the sound."

Struck on its hinge on the wooden culling board, a healthy scallop gave off a solid little thud. An empty shell felt lighter and delivered a disappointing tinny sound. We hauled the drags again. Tiny eels came up with the grass and squirmed upon the culling board together with minute fishes. Big round quahogs came up now and then, and whelk shells inhabited by fiddler crabs. Methodically, we tapped our scallops on the board and tossed them into the basket. Often, I was unsure whether a scallop was good or bad. Once, certain I had a good one, I tossed it into the basket where it landed with a *plink* and the shells fell apart. Empty.

"Don't worry," said Oscar. "It isn't just a *no*-vice that makes mistakes."

I flipped the offending shell overboard where it sank slowly into the pellucid green water, the white inner shell visible halfway to the bottom. By the time we had culled through about half a dozen hauls, the wire basket was full. Oscar emptied it into one of the five full-size baskets. It did not quite fill it halfway. We finished our second drag and Oscar turned the boat around again. We worked an hour to fill the big bushel. A licensed shellfisherman is permitted to take five such bushels. Oscar had not gotten his limit since the season's opening day. Another drag came home on the winch head. We went back to work.

By nine o'clock, the sun was shining down on the little fleet of scallopers. There were 18 boats towing their drags this way and that over the bottom of Cape Poge Pond. We had little time to watch them. There was always another cull, waiting.

"How are you doing?" Oscar asked me.

We were warm and dry and the temperature had climbed to about 40 degrees. The wind had remained northwest but was gentle, three knots perhaps. All in all, conditions seemed ideal. I began to wonder what it would have been like to do this work in a vessel rigged only for sailing, on days when three knots of wind would have been inadequate for the job.

It took more than a light breeze to keep a sailing catboat moving as it pulled its drags along the bottom. The only surviving contemporary account of a catboat scalloping under sail was discovered more or less by accident in the files of The Catboat Association. It was not very detailed.

"The men work in open boats in winter. Sometimes the temperature is near zero, a bitter wind may be blowing and their clothes may be soaked and frozen. Therefore, in the winter, scalloping is attended by hardship."

The article apparently came from a Nantucket newspaper. It noted that nine A.M. was the starting time, that eight bushels of scallops were allowed per boat, that licenses cost one dollar, and that the boats generally returned home by one in the afternoon. The latter would seem to indicate that the scallop population is no longer what it was, since modern methods and longer hours are no guarantee of even five bushels.

The whole notion of scalloping under sail in a catboat is so foreign these days that few men besides Oscar know anything about what was involved. Even Oscar never actually did it. According to him, the catboats towed from three to 10 drags, the forward drag being made fast to the mast.

"Mostly," he said, "the fishing was done going to windward. If the fishermen got off the scallops or reached a place where they couldn't go any farther, such as shoal water or underneath a beach, they would run her off before the wind. The fishing was usually done in a specific area and always on the same tack, depending on the wind direction. The drags were always set from the same side of the boat. They'd tack up and run back and they'd always haul all their drags before making a new set. Since wind was needed for this work but the fishermen couldn't be picky about the amount of wind, they often had to reef the sail and go out on cold, windy winter days."

Impelled by her steady Lathrop, *Vanity* plowed steadily back and forth over the scallop beds while we, her crew, gave no thought to tacking or reefing a sail. Those minutes when the drags were in the water gave us time to look briefly around at our competitors. Several of the boats had a wife or girlfriend on board doing the culling, while the skipper, hand on the throttle of a big outboard, guided the boat back and forth. Sometimes a boat came overly close to *Vanity*, but Oscar pretended not to notice. It was apparent that the other fishermen knew Oscar and that some were watching where we did our dragging. Oscar's renown for finding "quality stock" has spread farther than his fellow fishermen. Once, when President Kennedy wanted to serve a real New England dinner at the White House, the scallops came from Oscar and *Vanity*.

"Sometimes," he said, "after a near miss, a feller will get pretty upset out here and let you know it. But back on shore, he'll be as nice as anything." He wound a line around the winch head and another drag came on board. We started culling through its contents. As we worked, a sweet scent came down to us on the wind.

"Smell like marijuana?" asked Oscar.

"Smells like."

We cleared the culling board and Oscar upended another drag onto it. We worked through it fast with our gloved hands but found fewer than half a dozen scallops that were keepers. The "seed scallops," less than two inches long, we threw back. The morning wore on, evoking an article about scalloping published earlier that month in the *Boston Globe*. It said that scalloping was "easy money for men with good backs, big forearms and a small boat." A skiff plowed past, a woman in yellow foul-weather gear furiously working at the culling board, the man hunched at the tiller.

"How's your back?" asked Oscar.

Somewhere, low down, I was beginning to remember my back. "Fine," I said.

He brought another drag aboard. There were enough scallops in it to fill the fourth bushel basket halfway. After all his years of fishing aboard his catboat, Oscar's back is still fine. It is the sciatic nerve in his right leg that bothers him. It's OK in the boat but acts up when he stands for several hours in a little room at the end of his garage, opening the scallops. The room is a neat and clean place and Oscar has even waxed the bottled-gas heater set into the wall.

"I have to stand there for three or four hours, in the same place," he said, "to open the stock. The pain can get intense. I stood this as long as I could until I said, 'Well, there's easier ways than this.' I don't have to go, but I *like* to go."

His solution was to curtail his scalloping season by hauling *Vanity* in mid-December, long before the season ends in March, and carefully storing her beneath the trees.

By 11 o'clock, it was obvious that, whether he *had* to go fishing or not, Oscar was determined to bring home a limit catch. Slowly we began filling the last bushel and a half with clicking scallops. By noon, we had made our last drag.

"This," said Oscar, "is my first five-bushel day since opening day three weeks ago."

He tapped the throttle with a booted toe, handed over the tiller, and began cleaning the boat of grass and mud, using a little mop stored on the cabintop. The speedier, outboard-powered boats were ahead of us in returning, just as they had been coming out. Their owners, however, would have a bumpy ride home and would still have to clean their boats, although few seemed as concerned about keeping up appearances as did Oscar. We churned toward the narrow gut leading out into the harbor. *Vanity*'s propeller generates a lot of torque, and even with the board down to aid directional stability, it was necessary to mind the helm. I throttled back cautiously as we approached the docks 25 minutes later, but Oscar stepped in.

"You want to *boom* right in," he said, and I gave him the tiller. Then, with *Vanity*'s decks and cabintop gleaming in the midday sunlight and Oscar standing easily and confidently at the helm, the Lathrop churning smoothly, we *boomed* right in and landed like a leaf fallen softly to earth.

At the dock, we unloaded our gear and the five heaping bushels of scallops. While Oscar put his boat back on her mooring, I carried the scallops to the car. Each bushel weighed some 40 pounds, and I lifted each one carefully into the 50-year-old trailer that looked brand-new. When I was done, I placed the 50-year-old red gas can alongside them. By then, Oscar was back.

"Why, you're all loaded up," he said. "Did you use brute force or the wheelbarrow?"

He gestured to where a wheelbarrow, painted the same mauve color as the trailer, was nestled alongside a cottage. I looked down at the 200 pounds of scallops I had just finished loading.

"Brute force," I said regretfully.

"Then your back *must* be all right."

Now that we were ashore, we suddenly began to feel warm, and the scallops began to emit a pungent smell. We stripped off our oilskins and boots and sweaters. Then we got into the little Omni and drove up the scallop-shell driveway.

"Nellie," said Oscar, "will get us lunch."

The only time during which *Vanity* has spent longer than a few months out of the water was in World War II. Thomas Pease died in February 1941 and Oscar was drafted the following September. Along with most of the other young men from the Vineyard who now belong to American Legion Post 186, he was sent overseas. When that happened, he put *Vanity* under a tree in his yard and went off to England as wardmaster in a hospital unit. England is where he met Nellie.

Nellie Pease is a cheerful and talkative woman who keeps house as neatly as Oscar keeps his boat. She, however, doesn't have great enthusiasm for boats. The first time she went fishing with Oscar, he took her quahogging in Cape Poge Pond on a clear, cold day. While he raked for quahogs, which he did with the engine off, Oscar somehow forgot to plug *Vanity*'s exhaust with the special cork he used. The boat rolled just enough that day to let water enter the exhaust pipe and fill up the Lathrop's cylinders.

"I took out the spark plugs and turned her over to pump out the water," Oscar remembered, still incredulous. "Then I dried the plugs as best I could. But nothing would get that engine started."

By the time he gave up, it was twilight and cold and rough. *Vanity* was towed home by another boat, a happening larger than words that neither Oscar nor Nellie has ever forgotten. Now Nellie goes sailing with Oscar only occasionally, on bright summer days when the wind is not strong. But whenever Oscar sails off to a gathering of catboat enthusiasts, Nellie equips him with several tins of baked goods so that her presence is always felt, and savored, by all.

I asked Nellie how she felt when, as a new bride, she first came to Martha's Vineyard in 1946 and moved into the house with *Vanity* outside under a tree. "Oh," she said, "I thought the island was just awful. But soon I began meeting people and then I started my garden and everything was fine."

On the day that Oscar and I went scalloping, Nellie arose before we did. She set the kitchen table with white china and prepared a breakfast of eggs, homemade bread, and moist cake. When we got back home, she had made up a creamy chowder, full of sweet and tender scallops, and there were sandwiches and homemade apple cake besides.

"My," she said, "I did get worried this morning. The phone rang and it was the police chief and I thought you both had fallen overboard."

But the call was only to say the police had caught a boy who had been breaking windows near where Oscar kept his skiff, and the chief wanted Oscar to call him back.

"Well," said Oscar to Nellie, "as you can see, we didn't fall overboard and get drowned." He looked at me through his wire-rimmed spectacles and smiled. "After all these years," he said, "she still worries."

That night, the sun set in a profusion of reds. Along the road that leads north from Woods Hole, the trees stood out against the fiery sky as black silhouettes, and the lights in the little Cape-style houses looked warm and comforting. That night, Oscar had five bushels of scallops to look forward to opening. He would be standing in his garage for at least four hours the next day, deftly inserting his knife into the scallop shells and, with a wrist-flick, popping the creatures open. Secretly, I hoped he would not find many shells that were empty.

Five bushels of scallops would yield about 36 pounds of meat, then selling for $4.15 per pound. It was not an easy way for a man of 70 with sciatica in his leg to make some money, but Oscar was doing it merely because he has never done anything else. In another month, when the weather turned really cold and those who *needed* the money would have to go out whether they wanted to or not, Oscar would be at home eating Nellie's beef stew, dumplings, and pies, and *Vanity* would be secured beneath her tarps for the winter. It was an arrangement as natural as the seasons.

As I left Cape Cod behind me, I found myself thinking of a clear cold day in October when Townsend and Betsy Hornor had taken me and a small party of friends from Osterville to Edgartown aboard the Hornors' Dyer sportfisherman. We sped across Vineyard Sound, tied up in Edgartown, and strolled through the quiet streets and past Manuel Swartz Roberts's old place. Later, as we maneuvered away from the dock, we spotted *Vanity* lying on her mooring, and motored over.

"Hello, Oscar," boomed Townsend in a voice to make a bosun proud.

Oscar looked up and gave us a wave and we talked for a moment. Then Townsend backed away, pointed the bow for the harbor mouth, and cracked open the throttles. "That's Oscar," he mused, as we surged ahead.

I looked back. The last I saw of Oscar, he was kneeling on *Vanity*'s foredeck. In the autumn sunshine, patiently, meticulously, he was painting.

3

Uncle Bill and the Dolphin

T HE FIRST CROSBY WHO ever lived in Osterville was named Jesse. Nobody knows for sure when he moved there, but his son Daniel, born in 1765, presumably built boats in the village. Genealogists have done their best to draw a family tree based on his issue. As a genealogical exercise, the Crosby family presents an interesting challenge. There are tantalizing absences in birth and marriage records, and just enough similarity in initials, generation to generation, to keep one skeptical. There was, for instance, a C.W. as well as a C.H., but the former was Cornelius while the latter was Charles. There were two Horaces, three H. Manleys, at least four Daniels, a Herbert F., and a Herbert B. Many of these same Crosbys had nicknames, too. Wilton Crosby, who had a nephew and a grandnephew, Wilton B. and Wilton B., Jr., named after him, is still known to his descendants simply as Uncle Bill.

Wilton Crosby was born in 1856. His father was named Horace, and, like his father, Wilton became a boatbuilder. There were few male Crosbys who did *not* become boatbuilders. At one time there were five different Crosby boatshops, all more or less neighbors and all having the name Crosby as some part of their letterhead.

"Uncle Bill was brought up right here on the waterfront," said Wilton B. Crosby, Jr., "just like I was and just like the rest of them. They all just fell into boatbuilding naturally. It was the only thing to do."

Crosbys, it seemed, were born with an adze in one hand and a half-model in the other. Wilton started working in the shop run by his father and Uncle Worthington at an early age. There was no formal apprenticeship, probably nothing quite like

45

the more structured tutelage a boy might have gotten in later years at Lawley's yard in Quincy or at Herreshoff's in Bristol. "They just worked with the folks," said Wilton Junior.

The "folks" included carpenters, joiners, and painters. Mostly, they lived in Osterville or the immediate area, but sometimes a "hair-legger," a man from down the Cape, below the Bass River bridge, was employed, too. In 1900, when he was photographed with his crew, Wilton Crosby was employing six men. There is no way of knowing, anymore, how many boats Horace and Worthington Crosby built during their approximately 30 years of partnership. They could have turned out four or five a year, however, working the 10-hour days that then were considered normal.

At that time, the Crosbys' boats were built almost entirely of pine and oak, cut on Little Island just off the Osterville shore, and cedar, obtained anywhere possible. While the keel and stem were oak, the frames were made of rot-resistant pitch pine, sawn to shape from natural crooks. According to family records and to yachting historian W.P. Stephens, the Crosbys did not begin using steam-bent frames until 1892, when H. Manley Crosby bought a steam-powered saw and, simultaneously, decided to steam oak to replace the pitch-pine frames. The steam saw saved the builder the time of going to one of the nearby tidal-powered sawmills for the cutting of larger timbers.

"What could be more restful and fascinating," wrote Stephens, "than the slow forward movement of the great carriage on which the log was dogged as it hitched its way along, inch by inch, while the great saw, some eight inches or more in width with teeth two inches long, stretched tight in its vertical frame, moved slowly up and down, eating its way through the log?"

As business grew, the Crosbys lost their interest in such restful milling. Horace Crosby even lost some of his interest in boatbuilding. He retired from the shop at age 54 in 1880 and converted his house into an inn he called the Crosby House. Here, guests might spend an entire summer under the helpful, friendly care of Horace and his wife, Lucy, who was known as the "sergeant" at the Crosby House and who, according to Wilton Junior, "ran things with an iron hand."

Horace's retirement had little impact on the continuing production of Crosby catboats. Worthington took his own sons, Daniel and Charles, into the business. Another shop was run by Horace's eldest son, Herbert. Uncle Bill worked with Worthington until some time between 1878 and 1882. Then, when he knew he had enough experience, he set up his own cedar-shingled shop right next door to his Uncle Worthington's. There he began building catboats to the Crosby designs, using half-models as a basis for the lines and mold patterns. The boats were built heavily and ballasted with stones. Stems were stoutly constructed to support the big mast—30 feet tall for a racing 20-footer named *Magic* built in 1887—and the masts were made eight-sided on their lower portion so they could not rotate and would be well-supported where they emerged through the deck at the king plank. Much of the hardware was made by a West Barnstable blacksmith.

The shape of the Crosby boats, particularly those built before the turn of the century, was graceful, and the shape of those with counter sterns and underhung rudders was especially so. The hull lines show a firm bilge, rather hollow waterlines

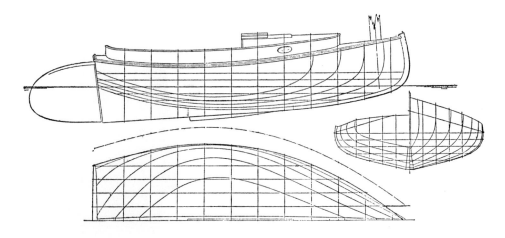

An H. Manley Crosby catboat of 1895. (American Sailing Craft *by Howard I. Chapelle)*

forward, and a beam carried well aft. The boats that differed markedly from this shape were the racing catboats, vessels built with reverse curves in bow and stern to present a comparatively short waterline, for measurement purposes, until they heeled. *Hit or Miss*, built by Herbert F. Crosby in 1893 for the catboat enthusiast with a bottomless pocketbook, Frank Randall, carried no such refinement but was fitted with a long and pointy "Gloriana" bow, which became fashionable after the success of a Nathanael Herreshoff 46-footer named *Gloriana*.

Frank Randall had so much success with *Hit or Miss* and his other Crosby boats that he commissioned Wilton to build him a new 25-footer. Uncle Bill slimmed down the beam below what a catboat normally would have carried and designed in enough bow overhang to bring the waterline down to the 20 feet required by the rules. He added spreaders and shrouds, in addition to a forestay, to support the mast. The resulting boat had a stretched-out look but she was fast. Randall won 10 races with this boat, named *Scat*, during the summer of 1896. He was by then so pleased with catboats in general that he helped finance the establishment of the Crosby Catboat and Yacht Building Company on Long Island, and installed Wilton's younger brother, H. Manley, as proprietor.

"I don't know," said Wilton Jr., "if he talked my grandfather into going down or just how it was, but down he went. They lived there on the Brooklyn side of the East River, on one of the Fall River Line boats that had been decommissioned and hauled ashore. In fact, my father was born there aboard the boat. My grandmother had enough after a while and told Manley he'd better buy her five tickets because she and the kids were going to head back to Cape Cod. And she did. He finally came later on."

Uncle Bill never moved from Osterville. He stayed in his shop and nothing much seemed to disturb his steady outpouring of boats. In 1893, he built one of the largest boats ever launched by a Crosby. This was the 45-foot *Nickerson*, made to order for two brothers who fished out of Chatham. When they found they could not

Wilton Crosby, 1856-1935.
(Courtesy Wilton Crosby, Jr.)

get along, they traded the boat back to Uncle Bill for two smaller ones. Over the years, the *Nickerson*, which made regular trips to Georges Bank, appeared with a number of rigs. It is uncertain now whether the boat was ever intended to be purely a cat-rigged vessel, or whether she was in fact a sloop.

In 1900, when Manley Crosby left New York to follow his family back to Cape Cod, he and Wilton became partners. Manley built a new shop next door to Wilton's, and they erected a milling shop in between. After that, the brothers cooperated closely. A 14-foot catboat ordered from Uncle Bill in 1908 for $300 was, in fact, built by Manley.

"It didn't seem to much matter," said Wilton Jr., "who built what. If one was busy, the other would fill in. That's just the way they did it."

The Crosbys' reputation spread through word of mouth, articles in the yachting press, and racing successes. It was common, too, for family members to cruise about the Cape, showing off their latest handiwork and generating lively interest among potential buyers. Uncle Bill was particularly skilled at this.

"He was a fella," said Wilton Jr., "that was good with people. He always dressed nice and wore a yachting cap. He was a nice fella, a fella who had some class."

There was something odd in the middle of Fishers Island Sound—a shape, a blob, a square of white out there in the water. It did not look like any of the more

Dolphin, *close-hauled.*
(Stan Grayson photo)

common navigational aids, or even any of that vast variety printed in full color in the navigation sections of sailing texts. I was squinting off at the white thing when Adrian Lane asked me if I'd like to take the wheel of his 21-foot catboat as we tacked our way out of Noank, Connecticut, in a light breeze.

Ghosting along in the zephyrs and eddies, the boat seemed perfectly balanced, and stayed that way until the sheet was trimmed too much. Then she more or less stopped. "Catboats are positive, aren't they?" said Lane, who is a bona fide sea captain, after I had eased the sheet again. "If you do something wrong, it's immediately apparent."

As we came about again, he continued his modest discourse. "She won't tack through 100 degrees always but she will tack through 80 degrees if she's strapped down in *smooth* water. There aren't too many marconi boats that'll do *that*." He said he thought the boom had been longer once and was sure the gaff had been longer. Those two differences, together with a full-size centerboard—the board had been cut down when the engine was installed—must have made for even better performance. But Lane is not disappointed. A week earlier, he had won first in his class in a local race during which the wind had been just strong enough *not* to require a reef, and all the legs but one were reaches. "It was," said Lane, "just elegant for catboats."

After a couple of tacks more, we were out of Noank and into Fishers Island Sound, and *Dolphin* was moving easily through the water, like a lazy fish. We settled back against the high coamings and enjoyed ourselves, savoring the idea that the boat had been sailing this way for what seemed an awfully long period of time. *Dolphin* was 65 years old. She had been launched in Osterville in 1917 by Wilton Crosby.

"This boat," said Lane, "has seen some things."

Nobody seems to know anymore who first ordered *Dolphin*. She was purchased some time in 1932 by an Edgartown fisherman named Joseph Mello, who had owned a smaller, Manuel Swartz catboat. He soon turned *Dolphin* to shellfishing in the fall and sailing parties in the summers. Oscar Pease remembers distinctly that Mello took excellent care of the boat. He fitted the cabin with curtains "all draped and made special and had caps for the coamings lined with flannel so the varnish would not be scratched." He also made canvas covers to protect the staving in the cockpit and the sole.

"I don't know how he worked with that boat when nobody else figured they could work their gear quick enough because they figured it would catch up on those things," said Oscar. "A rope might catch on this or that, and so forth, and then things would go overboard." Oscar remembers with wonder and respect Joe Mello's ability to keep a working boat looking like a yacht.

Mello owned the boat for many years and still was actively using *Dolphin* at the time she was driven ashore into a stone abutment during the great storm of 1954. *Dolphin* suffered extensive damage to her starboard side, and Mello, together with his brother-in-law, hauled the boat home for repairs. "They put her back together the only way they knew how," said Oscar, "which for them meant more like housebuilding than boatbuilding."

For five years thereafter, Mello used *Dolphin* for fishing and for daysails in pleasant weather with his wife, Mary. When he was too old to use the boat anymore, he sold her to Captain Bob Douglas, owner of the cruise schooner *Shenandoah*. "He brought her to my yard on a trailer for some rebuilding," remembered Douglas, "and he had tears running down his cheeks when he sold her." Five years later, the old fisherman died.

Bob Douglas did not keep *Dolphin* long. He bought himself a larger catboat built by Daniel Crosby and sold *Dolphin*. The man who bought her was John Killam Murphy, 85-year-old sailor, veteran of the Spanish-American War and World War I, Yale grad, longtime broker for John Alden, and a respected dean among East Coast yachtsmen. Murphy had owned an assortment of other boats, including yawls, ketches, sloops, and a 43-foot schooner, but he seems to have spent more time in the five catboats he owned than in all the others put together.

Some years later, looking back on his purchase of *Dolphin*, Murphy reflected that, "I probably never should have bought her, but I did have fun rebuilding her although it was rather expensive." He was able to sail the boat for four years before he came to the conclusion that he should sell her. By then he was spending most of his time aboard just tinkering or taking an afternoon nap in the cozy cabin. He placed an ad for the boat in *Yachting* magazine and informed the corresponding secretary of The Catboat Association, Ned Watson, of his decision. Watson had been mate of the Mystic Seaport schooner *Brilliant*. The boat's captain was Adrian Lane.

"I was offered the job by Briggs Cunningham when he was connected with the Seaport," said Lane, "and I took it." He paused as if remembering his association with the race car enthusiast and America's Cup skipper. "He was," said Lane, "a wonderful angel to have there."

John Killam Murphy was 90 when he sold his boat in 1965 to Lane and Watson, who bought *Dolphin* as partners. "John was acquainted with us," Lane remembered. "He wanted somebody who would take care of the boat, and Ned and I could do that."

Watson remembered *Dolphin* as being "tight as a tick" when he and Lane purchased her, but that was mainly because she had been sailed so infrequently. Once the boat was put into regular use, her old planks began to work and she began to leak.

"My wife," said Lane, "pumped Long Island Sound through the son of a bitch several times."

For all of his life, the village of Noank has been home to Adrian Lane. The house he owns today is the one he lived in when the storm of 1938 struck Noank. The house survived, barely, but the wind permanently altered the relationship of a pear tree and a pine tree in the front yard. They lean in opposite directions, as if trying to avoid each other. The storm was the end of Lane's very first catboat, a 16-footer. He took the boat into Mystic to ride out the blow, but a big steam yacht broke loose from its mooring and cut the catboat neatly in half.

"There was not enough left to do anything with," said Lane.

What was left was Lane's commitment to boats and the sea. His father had other boats built, and Lane sailed them and took note of every vessel of consequence, and some of apparently no consequence, that he saw. After he graduated from Trinity College, he never had a job that did not somehow involve boats. He served in warships in the Pacific and commanded an icebreaker in Greenland. Besides his time as master of the schooner *Brilliant*, he skippered the 141-foot sailing vessel *Atlantis* for the Woods Hole Oceanographic Institution and commanded various other research vessels, something he still does part-time. Once, he worked for Electric Boat, commanding an old boat full of sound-detection gear used for locating underwater noise. Submarines would circle his ship while switching on and shutting off machinery, and Lane's crew would try to identify each sound and determine what needed to be made more quiet. One night in the middle of January, a plate in the main hold ruptured and the boat sank right on the spot 200 miles off Block Island. Lane and his crew were rescued by a Norwegian bulk carrier after 26 hours in a life raft.

All this experience suited Adrian Lane for some unique jobs. He once served in the *Mayflower* replica, sailing the boat around Cape Cod Bay for several days while a film crew shot pictures for the television series, "The Saga of Western Man." At

Captain Adrian Lane.
(Stan Grayson photo)

the time, *Mayflower* was steered by the same whipstaff arrangement that had guided the original. The whipstaff was replaced with a wheel for the replica's transatlantic passage.

"The thing worked like a charm," said Lane of the whipstaff, a vertical shaft affixed to the tiller. "To go to starboard, you push to starboard. It was easy. It didn't take long to figure out the lines, either. She was slightly different from the original, which didn't have footropes on the yards. We had her out in a force 6 breeze, a good breeze of wind, and we had her down to the lower courses and the lateen mizzen but no topsails and we were just drowning the towboat that was astern of us. We were sliding along at seven knots, as steady as a church."

Mayflower's performance did not surprise him. He has never believed that old-fashioned ways are necessarily inferior to modern ones. He theorized that the little ship's high stern was intended to help *Mayflower*, and others like her, take care of herself when lying ahull, keeping her bow to the wind with no sail on.

"I asked Alan Villiers if it was supposed to work that way," he said, "and he said, 'Yes, it did.' They were not dumb in those days."

By the time Lane finished telling about the ungainly looking *Mayflower* scooting along wonderfully in a breeze, we were halfway across Fishers Island Sound and the white thing began definitely to look like a marshmallow.

"When we were kids," said Lane, "we used to come screeching back from Fishers Island at night half gassed. How we missed all these bricks, I don't know."

A sudden glint, a bright reflection of light, revealed the marshmallow to be a flying bridge. Beneath the white shape was an entire sportfishing boat that had torn her bottom out on a rock and sunk.

"You've got to watch the bricks out here," said Lane, "when the tide is running."

There was little chance of our putting *Dolphin* on the bricks. Lane has been sailing the Sound since he was a child. He knows the way the tides work and remembers every marker that has marked those waters since his childhood. He remembers the nest ospreys once built atop a spindle at the mouth of Noank's harbor, and how the birds nesting there made a good fog signal. After a lifetime of sailing the Sound, he still appreciates it. "Sometimes I come out here and just have a can of beer and get underway. I'm not gonna find any prettier scenery to look at anywhere."

Having had experience in boats of so many types, Lane has found complete contentment aboard his 21-foot catboat. "Anything bigger," he said, "would be too damn much trouble, too much bother."

He has worked hard at improving *Dolphin*. Every year there has been one job or another to perform, most of them major. He's had a new rudder built, a new centerboard, and a mast made from a schooner yacht's spinnaker pole. He investigated a planking problem and found that the fasteners Joe Mellow had used when making his repairs were too short. "They only went *that* far into the frames," he said. There was perhaps three-eighths of an inch between Lane's gesturing thumb and forefinger. The offending screws were plucked out and replaced by boatnails. The original nails driven by Wilton Crosby "couldn't be gotten out to save your soul."

One year, Lane's son refastened the boat's bottom, stopping most, but not all, of the leaks. *Dolphin* had, in fact, developed a fairly recent leak that Lane could not locate. He guessed it was at the hood end of the planking but decided it was nothing to be too concerned about, unless you think 200 to 300 strokes per week on the

Dolphin *reaching in light air, Fishers Island Sound, August 1982. (Stan Grayson photo)*

bilge pump that empties into the centerboard trunk is worthy of concern. He added floor timbers in the customary way of Noank boatmen, who, he said, like a floor timber for every frame, something the Crosbys did not believe necessary. The main thing left to replace on *Dolphin* was the keel. With this substantial exception and some suspect portions of canvas on deck and cabintop, *Dolphin* is now as sound as she's been since Lane and Ned Watson bought her.

As we picked our way slowly home through the moored boats in Noank, Lane offered his thoughts on why people are attracted to catboats. "I have this theory," he said. "The cabin of a catboat gives you a wonderful sense of security because there is just sitting headroom and it's comparatively small. I think it's a suppressed desire to return to the womb. I really think so. Anyhow, I think I'm more comfortable in that confined space than I would be in a modern sloop."

He has noted with curiosity *Dolphin*'s effect on some of his friends. One, a genuine shipping magnate who could afford to buy and discard a new boat each year if he desired, cruises with Lane on a fairly regular basis. "Somehow he likes catboats in general," said Lane, "and he's fascinated with this one in particular and likes going out in it."

Wilton Crosby retired from boatbuilding around 1930, some 13 years after he launched *Dolphin*. He continued to do some sailing, skippering a Wianno in the intensely competitive races held around the Cape, but mostly he devoted himself to running the Crosby House established by his parents. He proved just as successful an innkeeper as a boatbuilder and managed the place until he died in the old, tree-shaded house where his grandnephew lives today. Uncle Bill's son Harold took over the Crosby House after his father's death in 1935. He was the only Crosby of his generation who never became a boatbuilder.

Uncle Bill built his boats to last, and he knew they would outlast *him*, but there was no way he could have guessed at the long, happy life of the boat now owned by Adrian Lane, or the very special meaning it would come to have for catboat enthusiasts everywhere. In 1975, the steering committee of The Catboat Association decided an award should be created for annual presentation to a person of exceptional service to the organization. A highly skilled modelmaker named Don Rosencrantz was commissioned to make the award, which he constructed with the same skill and care that he devoted to his models in the Smithsonian Institution.

Each year, the recipient hangs the award, which is mounted in a varnished oak case, on his wall. The model is a gleaming replica of the catboat Uncle Bill Crosby built so many years ago. An engraved brass plaque identifies it. It is the *Dolphin* Award.

4

The Monument

THE FIRST TIME I met Ken Mapes, he was standing in the cockpit of his old catboat, guarded by two shrill dachshunds. He was a slender, blue-eyed man wearing a T-shirt and khaki shorts, for this was one of those steamy afternoons that occur frequently at the Jersey shore in July. Mapes had a tape measure in one hand and a pencil in the other.

"How long have you been working on her?"

"This must be about the fifth year," he said. He looked down at one of his dogs as if expecting some further clarification of this time factor. The dog sat down on the varnished steering box and stared at me.

Quickly, I scanned the boat. Everything below the sheer looked like trouble. The paint was peeling and the caulking hung down here and there, desolate gray strands that drooped into the yellow weeds. Yet the boat was obviously extraordinary. The coamings had been curved by an artist's eye, and there was a kind of able-bodied but comfortable tubbiness about the hull. There was beauty there, locked into the gray-brown cedar planks.

I seemed to have about two dozen questions forming all at once, but it was plain to see that the man in the T-shirt was busy. I imagined him being interrupted in his work by dozens of curious people.

"I guess you better go back to work."

"Fine," he answered, "but do stop by for a visit sometime."

That was the summer of 1975, but I made it a point to visit again that year, and again in all the years that followed.

There are not many places in New Jersey anymore with the look and atmosphere of David Beaton and Sons. It is a time warp sprawling amid the marsh grass at the very head of Barnegat Bay. This is not a glossy marina. It is an old-fashioned *boatyard*, little changed from the way it was in the 1930s when David "Pop" Beaton, a Scottish boatbuilder, bought the property. With his own hands, he built a tiny house in nearby Bay Head where he raised 14 children, and a big shop by the water where he built and repaired boats of all sorts, becoming in the process a legend in his own lifetime.

That the buildings here tilt a bit is self-evident. For a number of seasons, so did the docks. For years, a few of them remained canted at odd angles, heaved up by the ice of a hard winter that froze the bay solid. Old wooden boats are scattered around Beaton's like abandoned dreams. Now and then, one changes hands, and the new owners set to work. They think not of New Jersey but of distant seas, and of gleaming topsides rather than rotted planks and frames that need to be replaced, each new plank spiled, cut, beveled, fastened, and caulked, each new frame steam-bent into place and secured to the keel. It is a story played out anew each year, but not many people fulfill the dream.

Before 1970, Ken Mapes had never been to Beaton's boatyard. Then, one gusty November afternoon, he capsized his Barnegat Bay sneakbox near the Throgs Neck Bridge. By the time the boat was upright again, the gaff jaws had been broken. Rather than entrust the repair to just *any* yard, Mapes decided to take the spar back to those who had built it. That was how he happened to drive down to Beaton's one winter afternoon when the breeze blew hard from the west and the sky was the color of badly weathered teak.

Mapes remembered his first visit to the boatyard in a way most of those familiar with the place would recognize. "I *wandered*," he said.

Among the first things Mapes saw as he wandered was an old catboat. It squatted in the weeds, and even a casual glance revealed rot speckled fairly liberally around the cockpit staving and cabin. Whatever material covered the decks had cracked, and the canvas on the cabintop was split. A picture developed in color in Mapes's imagination, but it had little to do with the boat he was looking at.

Ken Mapes at Beaton's, 1981.
(Marie Darling photo)

"Right away, the boat's lines entranced me," he said. "I thought I recognized this as a Fenwick Williams catboat."

Mapes carried his sneakbox gaff into the yard office and talked about its repair with Pop Beaton's son Lally. Somehow the conversation drifted to the old catboat outside. The boat's sixth owner had recently passed away, and Lally Beaton believed the little vessel was for sale. The friends who had accompanied Mapes to New Jersey began urging him to buy the catboat and restore it. Mapes went back outside and looked at the boat again. This time, the picture he formed was more realistic.

"I saw possibilities of what that boat could become," he said. "But I certainly had no thoughts of buying it. It was a forlorn mess, even just looking at the outside. Inside, it was even more of a mess."

Fenwick Williams once told me that he could still remember drawing catboats in the margins of his textbooks instead of doing his schoolwork. He recalls, however, that by the time he joined John Alden's design office in 1923, it was a disaster to be known as a professional catboat designer. So, each day, he boarded the train from Marblehead to Boston, went to work, and designed yachts of all sorts, both power and sail. On occasion, Alden would remark to nobody in particular that Williams "draws lines just the way I want them!" This is a thought-provoking statement considering who worked in the Alden office while Williams was there. They included, to name just a few, Samuel Crocker, Murray Peterson, Charles MacGregor, and Carl Alberg. John Alden did not want those who worked for him working on their own designs while at the office. It was at home, therefore, mostly on his own time, that Williams began seriously to design catboats.

His first catboat plans were for an 18-footer; they were drawn about 1930 and published in *Yachting* the following year. "The boat is one of the great family of Cape Cod cats," said *Yachting*'s report, "that sturdy breed which can face rough water and strong breezes with confidence. . . . Only those who have had catboat

Fenwick Williams at his drawing board, spring 1983. (Stan Grayson photo)

experience can realize how much fun can be had in these craft, with but a single sail to handle, and draft enabling one to poke around in all sorts of little nooks which are quite inaccessible to the ordinary cruiser. Two people can have a whale of a cruise in a boat like this one."

A 21-footer was drawn next, followed by a 25. By the mid-1930s, Williams had essentially completed his catboat work, but it made such an impression on cruising catboatmen and armchair sailors that many believed he must have specialized in catboats all his life. These boats are all similar, exhibiting fullness in their sections from bow to stern, gracefully curved coamings and cabin sides, a sweeping, somewhat exaggerated sheerline, and moderate sail plans. They are known for their seakeeping ability and for a pleasing balance that has eluded many catboats.

"People credit me with designing a lot of catboats," Williams mused in his soft-spoken way, "but it always seemed to me that I just did one design in different sizes. I knew what I wanted for a catboat, what I thought was best."

The boat at Beaton's was indeed a genuine Williams design, one of the 21-footers. Lally Beaton told Ken Mapes that the boat had been built in 1946 in Petersburg, New Jersey. This made her one of several launched in the state at about that time, the rest having been built by the Johnson brothers in Bay Head. Mapes listened to all this and remembered another Williams-designed catboat he had sailed as a boy during summers in Wellfleet on Cape Cod. This decrepit boat at Beaton's, called *Nip and Tuck*, brought back pleasant memories.

By the time the sneakbox gaff had been repaired, Ken Mapes's resolve not to buy the catboat was, for no coherent reason, wavering. One day, he found himself arranging for a survey. The surveyor pointed out the boat's problems, but he did little to discourage Mapes.

"He just *flipped* over what he saw. He was *excited* by what he saw. He told me the builders, Toth, had a reputation for building very fine powerboats but he had never heard of them making a sailboat. He said it would cost $25,000 to replace the boat."

After the survey, Mapes tried to talk himself out of going any further. He was not sure he wanted to create a whole new lifestyle for himself and his dogs. Somehow, he slid into negotiations with the owner's widow. There was a debate about whether the Shipmate stove would be included with the boat, for the widow said her grandchildren would like the stove.

"No stove," Mapes heard himself saying, "no boat."

By then, the widow knew she had sold the boat, even if Mapes was not yet aware of it. Somewhat reluctantly, he paid the asking price—the same, he learned later, that the widow's husband had paid when the boat was in sound condition—and became the boat's seventh owner. Mapes promptly renamed the catboat *Dorothy Anne*, after his mother. He built a ridgepole to support a boat cover and immediately began spending all his weekends aboard. He drove down from Manhattan in his Ford station wagon, which he loaded with an ever-increasing collection of tools and materials. When he got to Beaton's he huddled in the cabin with his tools and the two dogs, Grafin and Victor, and went to work.

It was the winter of 1970, and another dreamer was in part-time residence at Beaton's boatyard.

Despite the surveyor's warnings, Mapes was unprepared for what he found when he himself began digging into his old boat. A recording engineer by profession, his woodworking experience was limited to little more than cabinetry made in his apartment. Now he faced a project that grew in complexity with each probe of his pocketknife. There was good news and bad news. The good news was that the hull, built of Jersey white cedar over oak, was basically sound. The bad news was all the rest. That and a budget that even precluded buying the quantities of Git-Rot Mapes believed he needed to exorcise the decayed areas. Without giving the matter much forethought, he removed all the caulking from the port side. After that, the winter wind blew cold through the old wooden planks.

"Oh," said Mapes of that first winter, "it was *bad*."

Right from the start, Mapes decided he was going to need a lot of pure cussedness to see the job through. He quickly devised a philosophy of rebuilding. "A thing I tried to do right from the beginning was to look at a condition and try to understand or figure out what had brought on the deterioration in the first place. I wanted to devise ways to keep it from happening again."

At the bottom edge of the cabin bulkhead, he found rot where the vertical staving joined the frames and floor timbers. Moisture had run down along the tongue-and-groove staving and had settled. "There were passageways for all the rainwater in the world to run down there and affect that oak. The same problem existed all around the cockpit staving. The cockpit sole was springy, rot-riddled."

When Mapes began looking beneath the cockpit sole, he found that someone had once overlaid the entire surface with plywood, apparently hoping that, by doing so, the rot would go away. Pondering the problem in the cold beneath the boat cover, Mapes decided to gut the cockpit entirely, and that is where the restoration of the *Dorothy Anne* really began. As soon as he began taking the cockpit to pieces, Mapes confronted the first of a hundred considerations basic to every stage of the rebuilding: The boat was not level. Getting things vertical, or at right angles, was going to take some thinking.

"In the cockpit," Mapes remembers, "I decided to keep the forward and after crossmembers of the sole in position and set the others in place using these as guides. Then I used the new crossmembers as a reference to finally position the new forward and after pieces."

It was a year before the new cockpit sole with all its bracing and the new main bulkhead were installed. February of 1971 found Mapes on his hands and knees under the boat cover, with two electric heaters. He was putting a layer of Dynel cloth and resin on the sole. He chose redwood for the bulkhead and cockpit staving, ripping the wood to size on the saw Pop Beaton let him use. Mapes did not enjoy working with the redwood, for it split and splintered easily, but it is intensely rot resistant, and it was affordable.

Early on in the rebuilding, he began seeking his own ways of solving problems of materials and methods. Rather than replacing all the staving in the cabin trunk, he drilled many holes into the staving at an angle. Then, instead of using Git-Rot, he filled all the holes with thinned resin from an oilcan. It was a messy business, but it worked. He built berths and lockers and obtained a number of antique oil lamps that he mounted in appropriate places. The interior developed in a way quite different from any other boat of this design. "The architect often leaves the layout

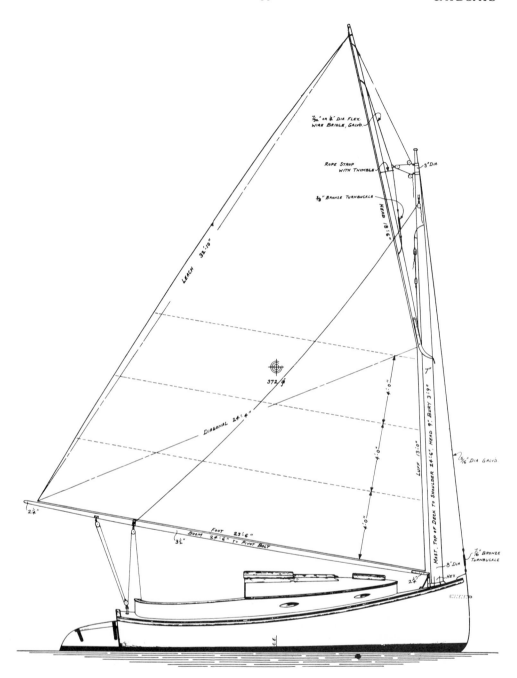

Sail plan of Fenwick Williams's 21-foot Cape Cod cat. (The Catboat Association Bulletin, Number 46)

below to the individual," said Mapes. "I didn't feel I was tampering with Mr. Williams's design."

Out in the cockpit again, Mapes roughly shaped two sheets of plywood to lay over the new crossmembers. He established a centerline on the plywood and proceeded to outline—full size—the placement of seats and the engine hatch. Then he cut out the parts he had drawn to use as patterns. He did this for the seats, engine hatch, icebox—installed to starboard in the cockpit—and the fuel and water tanks.

"I saw no help in doing this on a drawing board in scale," he said. "I did, however, make rough sketches of everything to be done anew, everything that was not merely copied from the original. Even if it was just a simple box for the steering gear, I'd sketch it first." He made a proper wheelbox, which the boat had not been given when she had been roughly converted from tiller to wheel steering. "Mr. Williams said the only mistake in the 21-footer was that he gave her tiller steering, originally, instead of a wheel." A new wheel was made for the boat by a retired sea captain named John Lindroth, whom Mapes always referred to as "a wonderful person and delightful man whose whole house is filled with beautiful furniture and stuff he built."

Mapes approached every stage of his work with an open mind—no preconceptions, notions, or hopes. "I learned to think like that," he said, "because every time I took something apart, I found something underneath that I didn't know about. Everything was new to me."

Dorothy Anne's decks were cedar. Although the wood was sound, the caulking was not. Someone had coated the decks with a liquid plastic, which had cracked and created "an unholy mess." Mapes got the plastic off with paint remover, creating an even bigger mess. Then he found he couldn't get the cotton out of the seams because the deck planks had been nailed laterally. He sanded the decks down to bare wood and forced the cotton back into the seams. Then he primed the seams with BoatLife primer and filled them with BoatLife compound. They no longer leaked.

Gradually, the work progressed. The old toerails, made of painted oak and lacking scuppers, had rotted. Mapes built new ones out of two pieces of mahogany spliced together before installation. He began a search for oak with which to make a new mast partner. The original had been made of four pieces, each a different width. It was so rotten that the boat's last owner had never dared remove the mast, fearing the partner might simply disintegrate if he did. Mapes made a new partner out of three pieces of oak.

Each time he completed one job, Mapes found another that needed doing. Sometimes, he had to do the same job twice. He took the cabintop down to bare wood and filled all the seams with a product recommended by the yard, called Famowood. Then he fastened a sheet of Dynel over the cabintop and coated it with resin.

"I cured the resin with Versamid," he said, "which renders the cured resin flexible. It's been pounded into my head that, in a catboat, everything works, including the cabintop. So I hoped that the flexible resin would eliminate any cracking."

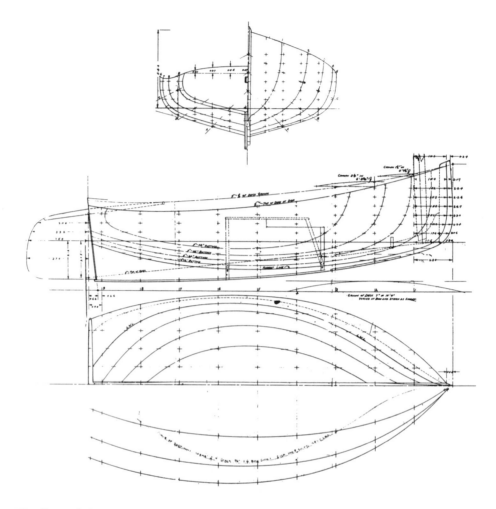

The lines of the Fenwick Williams 21-footer. (The Catboat Association Bulletin, *Number 46)*

But it didn't. The wood somehow absorbed moisture, then expanded and contracted and crushed all the Famowood in the seams. The Dynel split while *Dorothy Anne* lay in her cradle. Mapes went over each split with a disc sander, feathering the edges. Then he refilled the exposed seams with sawdust and resin and covered each split with a strip of Dynel, feathering the patches as he went. Finally, he put another layer of Dynel over the whole cabintop and applied two more layers of resin. The seams then apparently stabilized.

One day, Mapes began thinking about finishing the bulkhead behind his Shipmate stove with tile. He looked up "delft" in the Manhattan Yellow Pages and found one store in the city that sold the famous tiles.

"They must have thought I was a raving lunatic because I got so enthusiastic about what I saw," he said. "I suddenly realized I could do something nice back there."

He finished the bulkhead in blue-and-white delft tile, each tile picturing a sailboat or a windmill. He made up an elegant pair of louvered cabin doors and a hundred other things. Gradually, projects were completed and time passed. Summers gave way to autumn, autumns to winter. One winter, a blizzard descended, and Mapes spent his weekend shut up in the boat with his dogs and a pork roast that he cooked in a small electric oven. After each winter the spring came, and *Dorothy Anne* demanded more and more. Observers at the yard joked that the catboat was growing roots in the earth beneath her cradle. There was no end in sight, and Ken Mapes was learning the hard way what it really means to restore an old wooden boat. But in the process, he became a genuinely skilled craftsman.

Nowhere was this skill better reflected than in the center section of the boat's dropleaf table. There, Mapes inlaid his boat's name. "When I finished the inlays on the cabin table," he said, "I thought I'd show them to Pop Beaton. I went in and handed the thing to him and he sat there and looked at it. Then someone came in whom I did not know. Pop handed it to the man and said, 'See what I made.' Coming from a man I admired so much, I thought that was beautiful."

By the time Mapes had owned *Dorothy Anne* for several years, the boat had become as much a part of him as his pants and shoes. He thought about her wherever he went. He gave up smoking. He *lived* for the boat.

"I don't remember at what stage I was hired to engineer a recording of the Bible," he said, "but that could be awfully boring. You have to keep your mind on something else to keep your sanity, and thinking of the boat helped get me through that stage of my life."

Mapes went through the Bible three times with Alexander Scourby. He had only one agreement with the great recording artist. This was that work ended at one P.M. on Friday and did not resume again until Tuesday. Every Friday afternoon, Mapes loaded his Ford wagon and drove to Mantoloking with his tools and dogs, who never tired of dashing around *Dorothy Anne*'s decks or chasing the boatyard cat, which never lost the upper hand in this game. One year, Mapes, quite by accident, discovered that Grafin had gone blind. After that, the red dachshund stopped running around the boat. Mapes believed she was afraid he might leave her at home if she continued her antics.

In 1975, Mapes's work progressed to refastening and recaulking the entire hull, a process that took two years of weekends. By now, the catboat had become a sort of focal point for everyone who entered Beaton's. People seemed to gravitate to the boat until they stood in wonder beside the ample hull while the dogs barked and the owner tried to continue his work.

"I'd get so uptight and tense because I was trying to be polite but really dying to work," Mapes said of this attention. "The thing was I could sit and talk all day long because everyone here at Beaton's is here for the same thing and shares common interests. I think we're evaluated according to our boat, and a guy could be president of a big corporation but even he lets people know he's just a sailor like the rest of us. So we all have a common bond here."

Mapes was about finished with the hull work when Pop Beaton died in 1977. Pop had never been aboard *Dorothy Anne*, yet he had always seemed to know exactly what Mapes was doing. The old boatbuilder had touched many lives, and Ken Mapes knew how much he owed him.

"For one thing," he said, "Pop set an example of craftsmanship because anything he touched with his hands came out beautifully. He allowed me to use the shop and encouraged me with his generosity. Without all that," he waved his hand around *Dorothy Anne*'s cabin, "this couldn't have happened. It was Pop's own goodness that made it possible."

One of the inevitable questions that all visitors to *Dorothy Anne* would ask Ken Mapes was when he expected to launch his boat. His answers varied. Usually he was noncommittal. Sometimes he might say, "Next year." As the years passed, some regulars at the yard began wondering if *Dorothy Anne* would ever sail again. But Mapes never had any doubt about that. Time and again, he had seen new owners of old boats descend on Beaton's, and he had watched what happened.

Generally what happened was this: The owner would bring along a group of friends and the crew would begin working night and day. After a while, most of the helpers would disappear. The owner would keep at it, all the while planning his cruise to distant islands. This would continue until the time when reality would finally, irrevocably intrude, and the owner would understand that he had undertaken an essentially impossible project in terms of his own ability, time, and financial resources. Then he would disappear just as quickly as he had come, and the boat once again would be for sale.

"I saw that happen so many times," Mapes told me one day in the winter of 1980. With a shovel, he put more coals in the Shipmate stove. "I think that's one thing that kept me going. I never would have bought this boat if I had known what was going to be involved. But there was no way I was going to give up." By then, *Dorothy Anne* had been afloat for two seasons, hadn't leaked a drop, and, although sparless, had been plying the bay under the power of her Atomic Four. The engine was the only thing aboard that had required relatively little work.

It got him down to Abbott's Cove one summer day just in time to be rammed by a drugged teenager driving a jet-ski. Mapes tired of yelling at the youth when nothing he said had the slightest effect. Then the ridiculous vehicle struck *Dorothy Anne* on the port bow. Later, when Mapes approached a raft of boats manned by his friends, one of them blurted in shock: "Ken, you've got a hole in your bow!" Only the fact that the bow rode high without a mast in place kept *Dorothy Anne* from sinking right there in the cove.

"A lady cop came in and caught the kid," said Mapes. "He wouldn't talk and had tattoos. It was weeks before he confessed to his father."

Lally Beaton repaired the damage and Mapes's insurance covered the cost. By the winter of 1981, just over a decade after he bought his boat, Ken Mapes got down to the final job of stripping the spars and beginning their refinishing. He and others at Beaton's were mystified briefly by a line attached to the 10-foot-long gaff bridle. Mapes did some research in *The Catboat Book* and learned that the line was intended to adjust the bridle's effective length to accommodate sails of different cuts.

Dorothy Anne, *now* Emily L., *sails California waters in the hands of her new owner. "She outpoints most of the fancy boats on our bay," he reports, "and kills them off the wind." (Courtesy Frederick B. Newell, Jr.)*

"Fenwick Williams," he reflected, "sure knows what he's doing."

That spring Mapes began carefully filling a crack in the mast with flexible caulking compound. It was preferable to a hard filling, he believed, since it would allow the wood to work. For the first time in all the years since he had owned the boat, he was really permitting himself to look ahead to sailing.

"I want to anchor down on Tice's Shoal," he said, referring to one of the places left on the Jersey shore that has not been crowded with housing. "I have friends on the Cape too. The day this gal," he said, patting the boat, "gets up Wellfleet Harbor—that will be something."

A couple of months later, on a warm Sunday in spring, I drove down to Mantoloking to see what progress Mapes had made on his boat's spars. The boat was in her slip but nobody was aboard. When I asked around, I learned Mapes had been feeling poorly and had not been to Beaton's for a couple of weeks. When I called him, he said he was "having tests." Not long after that, he was admitted to Deborah Hospital, not far from Fort Dix in the Pine Barrens. I drove down to visit him. There were a lot of boat magazines and books in the room and all his friends from Beaton's had been there to visit. He lay on his bed and looked forward to getting back to work.

"What I really want," he said, "is to have this black lump out of my lung."

The doctors conferred. They prodded and tested and determined that the condition was inoperable and sent Mapes home to New York and radiation treatment at Memorial Sloan-Kettering Cancer Center. He described it once as "a very scary place where most of the patients don't talk to each other."

The doctors told him, after some months, that they were very pleased with the progress being made in reducing the size of the tumor. Mapes began looking ahead to getting his strength back and getting down to the boat. There was so little left to be done and the dream of sailing down the bay was strong. Not long afterward, on the final day of 1981, Ken Mapes died suddenly at his New York apartment. The last time I saw *Dorothy Anne*, she was sitting in her cradle, awaiting a cross-country journey to California and a new owner. Pop Beaton's grandson Tommy came by. He looked up at the boat and shook his head.

"You know," he said sadly, "no matter who ever owns this boat, it will always be Ken's."

We both felt numb, I guess. I nodded my agreement and, as I did, I realized the boat was resting in almost precisely the same spot where I had first seen her, so many years before.

5

The Marvelous Dream of Nelson Hartranft

T HE TROPHY, AN ORNATE silver mug featuring an anchor and line in bas-relief, was made at Tiffany's in 1871. Commissioned by a group of New Jersey yachtsmen, it was awarded for the first time that July. Because it is still being presented today, it is generally considered to be the oldest purely *American* trophy in the sport. (The America's Cup was wrested from the British.) This old trophy is the Toms River Challenge Cup, and although sloop-rigged boats have won it from time to time, it has, over the past half-century, become firmly identified with the racing of large catboats.

In 1982, the annual race for the Toms River Cup was held in mid-July, and for the crew of the new racing catboat *Wasp*, things got off to a bad start. We had boarded the boat where she lay at anchor off the north shore of Toms River, just where the river emerges into Barnegat Bay. There were six of us in all, clambering aboard only 15 minutes before the start.

"Quick," said the boat's owner, Nelson Hartranft, "let's get her pumped out."

Because the electric bilge pump had not yet been installed, we pumped by hand. Boatbuilder Tommy Beaton and I went below. We put the flexible hose of the plastic bilge pump into the centerboard case, held it there, and took turns pumping what Beaton made clear was strictly rainwater. It was a hot day, and we were soaked with sweat almost at once. We pumped as fast as we could, cocooned in *Wasp*'s stripped interior, the oiled cedar planks smelling sweet and new, copper rivets glowing. Down below, we could not feel the force of the wind, which was considerable.

"Would this be a reefing breeze for *Wasp*?" I suggested.

Tommy Beaton is a quiet, soft-spoken young man. The most obvious things about him are his bright blue eyes and his modest way, both being traits that he shares with his father, Lally. Right then, he did not want to say much about the wind, which was gusting to some 18 knots, and he just pumped harder than ever when his turn came. The fact was, there was no time to reef even if we'd wanted to.

"Better come up from below there," someone called. "We've got to get going."

We put on our life jackets, required for all crewmembers when racing aboard the 28-foot-long A cats, and clambered out of the low-roofed cabin. The breeze started to dry us out at once.

"OK," said Nelson Hartranft, "let's get the sail up."

Around us, our three competitors were underway, big, low-sided marconi-rigged catboats swooping this way and that in the gray water. Three of us went to work on the green-and-white braided halyard, and *Wasp*'s sail, all 605 square feet of it, started up the 49-foot mast. It was a long haul. The last foot or so was swayed up taut with the halyard tailed around its cleat atop the cabin.

"That's not enough, not enough," said Hartranft's son, Nelson Jr.

We got the sail up another few inches, straining. There are no winches on an A cat. Tommy Beaton and I went forward to break out the anchor. That was hard work, too, but the boat lay in reasonably shallow water and we had only about 50 feet of anchor rode to pull in, hand over hand. By the time the anchor was aboard, the first gun had sounded and *Wasp* was in irons with less than a minute to go before the start. As the boat began to fall off, Hartranft ordered the centerboard down and the new board promptly stuck fast in the case. Someone grabbed a length of wood and pressed down on the board, and the next thing that happened was that the improvised tool became wedged between the boom and the centerboard.

"Damn," someone said.

Somehow, *Wasp* got underway, trailing the other A cats across the starting line by many, many boat lengths. Nelson Jr. took over the helm from his father. "Let's just concentrate on sailing the boat," he said. "We can make a race of this yet."

A puff hit us and we heeled over too far. Warm river water rushed along the leeward rail. "Ready about!"

Skip Moorhouse, the beefy sailmaker who had built *Wasp*'s sail, began hauling in mightily on the mainsheet, and we made ready to slack the running backstays, without which an A cat's mast would not stand very long. 'Round we came onto the new tack. It was not until we rounded the windward mark that we really began to suffer the consequences of whole sail. Then *Wasp* developed a strong weather helm and our helmsman began to tire. By the jibe mark, there was uncertainty about whether to risk a jibe or to tack. We jibed. The varnished boom, 36 feet long, came over with a whoosh.

For a while, it seemed as if we were gaining. In fact, we passed the black-hulled *Bat*, which Nelson Hartranft also owns. *Bat* was having a worse time of it than we were. She did not like being pushed in that wind and was leaking, seeming to shovel the water. We went by her with Moorhouse hanging on to the tiller with both arms.

"I thought it would pull my arms out," Nelson Jr. said later of his turn at the helm. "I thought it would break my bones."

At the start of the 1982 Toms River Cup race, Wasp *is in irons. Later, she leads* Bat *in rough going. (Jackie Pellaton photos)*

Next in front of us was the blue hull of *Spy*, and well beyond her, romping, was *Mary Ann*. We did not catch either boat, and at some point, the wallowing *Bat* elected to drop out before something serious happened. That was how *Mary Ann*, 60 years old that very day, won the Toms River Challenge Cup in 1982.

"That was the worst race I ever sailed," said Nelson Hartranft as we prepared to tow *Wasp* to her slip.

"Well," said Moorhouse, "the mistake was obvious, not reefing, but you know, I think this was a good thing for the class. The new boat didn't just run away with everything."

Hartranft agreed. He had won the Cup before, not to mention the Bay Championship awarded to the overall winner of the season's A cat series. He did not want to squelch competition with his new boat: He wanted nothing more than to revive interest in A cat racing. For a time, after we had tied *Wasp* up, we relaxed in the hot sun, drinking cold beer and sodas. *Wasp* had won her first race in light air, but nobody doubted then that a shakedown period would be necessary before boat and crew understood each other.

"I really learned a lot about this boat," said Moorhouse, who had been up late the night before reworking the sail. "It was more work than a big boat. It's an *enormous* 28 feet!"

Tommy Beaton said nothing, but it was clear that he was disappointed. He had spent too many hours—years, in fact—building the boat, and wanted her to do her best every time out. Yet he appreciated the idea that it would not be particularly constructive if *Wasp* walked away with first place each time she raced. There is an *aura* that goes with A cat racing, and nobody who truly cares for the boats would want anything to diminish that aura or harm the class.

When we had finished our drinks, we each went home thinking over the details of the race. In her next outing, *Wasp* made a strong comeback, winning, and she went on to win the Bay Championship. It seemed to me a special treat to sail aboard the boat. It is not every day that one boards a brand-new yacht that is, save for a Dacron rather than a cotton sail, identical to a boat launched 59 years previously (in 1923). Yet that is *Wasp*. She is like nothing so much as a brightly painted and varnished memento of an entire generation of American yachting. That she exists at all is either an accident of fate or something of a miracle, depending on how you look at things, for *Wasp* is essentially a reincarnation. She is the spirit of the *Tamwock*, a boat destroyed by fire more than 35 years ago.

The house where Ed Crabbe lives is a big cedar-shingled dwelling with white-painted window frames, overlooking a racing sneakbox on a marine railway in the yard. It is, in fact, a *boathouse*, but the living quarters over the enclosed slips are large, airy, and comfortable. The walls are wood-paneled and lined with good books. Impressively crafted ship models rest in glass cases on shelves or sideboards. One of them, a centerboard schooner, was designed for Crabbe's father by Charles Mower. For years, the schooner was moored in the river just off the boathouse. She was designed just two years after Mower designed the very first A cat in 1922. That A cat was *Mary Ann*, and Ed Crabbe's father was so impressed by her that he ordered the second boat in the class, *Bat*, shortly thereafter. *Bat* was built by Morton Johnson in Bay Head in 1923.

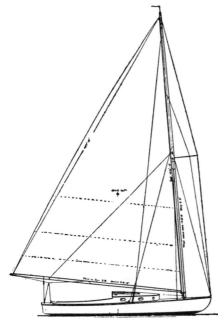

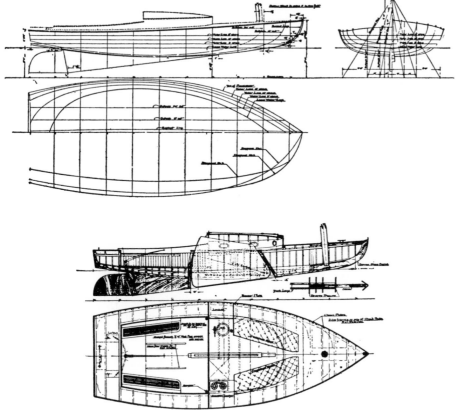

Sail plan, lines, and arrangement plan for Charles Mower's Mary Ann. *(Sailing Craft, edited by Edwin J. Schoettle)*

"It was natural," said Ed Crabbe, "for my father to go to Charlie Mower to design a new catboat. Mower had designed boats down in Barnegat Bay for years, including a radical racing boat for the mayor of Philadelphia that was 34 feet overall but just 18 feet on the waterline, and another boat that was the forerunner of the class E scow." Up in Ed Crabbe's boathouse, the ghosts of once-renowned old yachts are alive and well. He knows them all personally.

Charlie Mower was born in Lynn, Massachusetts, in 1880, and his son remembers that boats were, for Charlie Mower, "a pastime, vocation, everything." Mower built his first boat in his backyard and raced it at Marblehead and other ports around Boston. He began his career in Boston as a draftsman, first for Arthur Binney and later for Bowdoin Crowninshield. In 1899, he went to work for Thomas Fleming Day, the great editor of *The Rudder*, and began writing about boats and designing more seriously. It was Mower who created *Sea Bird*, the 25-foot yawl sailed across the Atlantic by Day and two companions. While with the magazine, Mower designed various racing yachts including a Sonder class boat that won the Kaiser's Cup in 1909 in a series sailed at Marblehead. He left *The Rudder* in 1911 to work full time as a yacht designer, and pursued a distinguished career until his death in January 1942.

Ed Crabbe, who sailed to Bermuda aboard his father's schooner with Mower, remembers the designer as "the nicest man you ever met, very quiet and unassuming, very knowledgeable about boats and yachting without pushing it at all. He was a top-grade gentleman." Crabbe still has a model of that schooner, *Shellback*, in the house. The model was built by Pop Beaton.

Charlie Mower designed five A cats, four of which survive. The boats possess subtle differences but are similar in most respects. Low-sided, with flat bottoms and soft bilges, they have large centerboards and a substantial skeg on which the underhung rudder is mounted. Originally, the boats were fitted out with berths and heads and were regularly cruised about the bay. The masts are secured by a pair of shrouds on either side, three forestays, and running backstays.

"Once, some novices were racing *Lotus*," said Nelson Hartranft of one of these Mower A cats, "and they were running before the wind with neither backstay set up. I couldn't believe what I saw. The mast had to be at least 30 degrees forward of the vertical, and we never knew why it didn't break."

Originally, the boats possessed a peculiar, short gaff at the sail's head. This "Swedish rig" was a kind of uneasy union of the traditional gaff rig and the new marconi sail, and it did not work particularly well. A true marconi rig was soon substituted.

According to Ed Crabbe, whose knowledge of the A cats is encyclopedic, *Bat*, the boat his father commissioned, is the most unusual of the surviving quartet because she possesses a rather canoelike bow, and because of her slightly longer waterline. *Mary Ann* and *Spy* developed reputations as especially good heavy-air boats, and *Spy* is known further for being very quick to windward but dead slow when running. *Bat* earned a reputation as a good all-around boat. A fifth A cat designed by Mower had a somewhat narrower beam than the others. Built in 1923, this boat, *Helen*, was not successful.

To build *Bat*, Crabbe Sr. traded in his catboat *Gem*, which had won the Toms River Cup in 1886 but was showing signs by the 1920s that the times were passing

Four A cats in the 1920s. Left to right, Tamwock, Mary Ann, Bat, *and* Spy. *(Courtesy Ed Crabbe)*

her by. When, in her first season, *Mary Ann* outclassed all catboats then racing, including *Gem*, Crabbe promptly signed a contract with Morton Johnson. The contract called for the builder to "provide all the materials for the hull and perform all the labor necessary for construction of a racing yacht about 28 feet as to specifications furnished by C.D. Mower.... By this agreement, cost shall be $1,600...." Crabbe's new boat won the Toms River Challenge Cup in 1925.

Because the Mower A cats have survived, it is Mower's name that remains most closely associated with the class. There were two other A cats, however. They were built in 1923 to designs by the quiet, piano-playing naval architect who later designed the famous Star class, Francis Sweisguth. The two Sweisguth boats were built in Toms River by John Kirk. One was called *Foresome*. Owned by a syndicate whose head was the wealthy Philadelphian Edwin Schoettle, *Foresome* is remembered as a failure by those who can recall anything at all about her. Walter Zwarg, whose family owned an aged champion catboat designed by A. Cary Smith, recalls that *Foresome* was "six inches shorter on one side than the other and was never properly rigged." Schoettle's son Carl thought the boat's mast was too heavy, ruining her.

The second Sweisguth catboat, however, was more successful. She was raced for many years until her destruction in the 1940s in an Island Heights boatyard fire. That boat, brightly varnished, was originally owned by a member of the Seaside Park Yacht Club named Larkin. Larkin named his boat Seagull but translated the word into the tongue used by the Indians who once had frequented the New Jersey coast. The name he chose was *Tamwock*.

Nelson Hartranft had wanted to own an A cat since he was a boy racing sneakboxes on Toms River. Almost every day, he saw the Crabbe family's *Bat* on her mooring. To a young, impressionable sneakbox sailor, *Bat*, or *any* A cat, was the epitome of yacht racing. At some point he cannot now recall, Nelson Hartranft promised himself that he would someday have an A cat of his own, and even in the lean years when he was establishing himself in business and could see the big catboats decaying inexorably in their winter cradles, he never forgot the dream. When he finally bought an A cat, it was not a new boat. It was old *Spy*, and she needed a lot of work. He got the boat in 1975 and took it to Lally Beaton for repair.

"Basically," Beaton said, "I learned that these boats all need work on the bow and on the garboard planks and around the butt blocks, because there is a tremendous strain on these parts."

Spy's weaknesses, induced by age and hard racing, were attended to by Beaton, and Hartranft won the Bay Championship in her in 1976. "What that did," said Hartranft, "it more or less whetted my appetite."

He got hungry for his boyhood favorite, *Bat*. She still existed in his imagination just as she had then, as *the* boat. *Bat* had her problems, but she was still in one piece, not a ghost. He had made a couple of fruitless efforts to buy *Bat* but she had gone instead to a syndicate in Island Heights. When the syndicate members began having disagreements, however, and when *Bat* began needing ever more expensive repairs, Hartranft at last bought the boat in August 1976.

"I made them an offer they couldn't refuse," he said.

When Hartranft finally acquired *Bat*, he sold *Spy*. Then, in rough going, *Mary Ann*'s mast drove down through her bottom. After an inadequate repair, Hartranft negotiated *her* sale to a friend of his with himself as co-owner. He was rapidly acquiring the entire A cat fleet. The two men took the boat to Beaton's for repairs.

"I remember telling 'em," Lally Beaton said in his soft way, "that I didn't want to do the job."

By the time *Mary Ann* appeared at his docks, Lally Beaton was tired of doing all the rough jobs everybody else ducked. He had already fixed *Mary Ann* once, at a time when she seemed too far gone to bother with, and he did not want to do it again. He resisted, but not for long.

"All these people have really got a feeling for these boats," he said. "In a weak moment, I said to myself, 'Well, I should really fix it because I'd hate to be the reason the class dies.' That was a big mistake because the next day, these two are back asking me again to fix the *Mary Ann*."

Two years later, in 1978, Hartranft became sole owner of *Mary Ann*. He had Beaton do further repairs, won the Bay Championship with her and sold her to another enthusiast. The only A cat he had not owned was *Lotus*, so he set out to buy her, too. By the end of the 1980 season, *Lotus* was leaking so badly that she had to be put onto the flats near the Seaside Park Yacht Club to keep her from sinking.

Tamwock under "Swedish rig,"
circa 1924. (Courtesy Ed Crabbe)

Hartranft bought her and took her to Lally Beaton. The boatbuilder looked at *Lotus* and saw another tough job that anybody else would duck.

"OK," he said, and agreed to a project that would require some two years' work.

Ever since he discovered that his sailing pal Snapper Applegate owned a partial set of Mower's plans for an A cat, Nelson Hartranft had been thinking of ways to convince Lally Beaton to build a new boat. Applegate had owned *Lotus* once, and had some drawings of *Mary Ann*. So Hartranft began asking Beaton if he might want to build a new *Mary Ann*. Just outside his shop, Beaton had about 400 reasons not to build the boat, 400 boats that needed to be maintained and stored. He said that he did not have time to build a new A cat and do his yard work, too.

Hartranft did not give up. With Applegate's plans and a set of fresh lines taken from *Mary Ann* or one of the other boats, Beaton would have a unique opportunity to recreate a part of history. But Beaton continued to refuse. He was worried enough that a rumor had somehow started that his yard was about to begin building the lovely little racing sneakboxes for which it had once been famous. He responded to Hartranft's idea about taking lines off an A cat as follows: "These boats are so out of shape that there's nothing really left to give a *true* set of lines."

Hartranft wondered where he could find a complete, original set of lines drawn by Mower or Sweisguth. He had given that up and was intently devising some new way to approach Beaton and skirt the issue of exact lines when a very surprising

Tamwock *(Courtesy Albert Diss)*

thing happened. Hartranft loaned his slip at a Toms River marina to a friend who
owned a large schooner. One day in late spring, one of the schooner's crew
wandered into a local antique shop. He idly pulled open the drawer of an old
dresser and discovered a large envelope. It contained plans for a sailboat. He
spread out the plans and began studying them, oblivious to anything else in the
store or to the traffic surging along just outside on Route 166. The plans, perfectly
preserved in the same envelope in which they had been mailed a half century
before, were for a 28-foot catboat. The boat's name was neatly lettered at the
bottom of the plans, right by the designer's name. "Tamwock," it read. "Francis A.
Sweisguth."

"Luckily, he knew something about sailboats," said Hartranft. "He took them to
a local engineering firm and had them copied." One of the first people to get the
plans was Snapper Applegate. He passed them on to Hartranft and *he* now had a
new lever in his talks with Lally Beaton. The next time he drove to the boatyard, he
carried the complete plans for an A cat in his briefcase.

Beaton still remembers Hartranft's enthusiasm with a kind of wonder. "He really
wanted to build it," he said. "Finally, I began thinking about my son Tom. I thought,
'Well, if he is going to go on in this business, the only way to learn is to participate in
the building of a boat, and an A cat is not a bad place to start.'"

Hartranft stayed right there, making strong pitches to the boatbuilder. He told

Beaton he could take as long as necessary to build the boat. Take three years, he said. If that wasn't enough, take *four*. Take as much time as it needed and do the job the best way possible. There wouldn't be any pressure from *him*.

Finally, Beaton wavered. After 35 years of repairing A cats, after all the back-breaking hours of doing the tough jobs nobody else would or could do, Lally Beaton decided to build an A cat of his own. He was going to improve it, too, where necessary, based on what he had learned from the other ones.

"It's amazing to me," he said, "that the boats have lasted as long as they have."

Looking at Sweisguth's old plans, he knew at once that *Tamwock* had not been designed with enough strength in the bow, under the mast, an area where tremendous pressure is exerted when the stays are tightened. He made the mast step 2½ inches wider and an inch thicker than what the plans called for. He added a pair of bronze straps that tied the bow together and helped spread the loads. Any modifications to Sweisguth's plans were aimed at a single goal, strengthening the boat. There was never any idea of changing the designer's basic plans or of making this new boat so different that she would, in effect, be a rule beater, thoroughly outclassing the old boats. Hartranft's most basic reason for having the boat built at all was to spur interest in A cats, maybe even to prompt somebody else to build one.

Sweisguth's plans called for floor timbers for each of the boat's 37 frames. Beaton bonded all the floor timbers to the keel with bronze angles through-bolted with tough ⅜-inch silicon bronze bolts. Previous A cats had been fastened with copper rivets, one reason, Beaton believes, they have held together for so long. He did the same on this boat, but had a hard time finding copper nails to use.

"It used to be," he said, "that you could go to any of your dealers and buy a keg of nails. We went to a big supplier and he told me that he had exactly five pounds of copper nails. Eventually we got what we needed, but it took time."

After the floors had been installed, together with the centerboard trunk, the molds were added, followed by the ribbands, those long stringers running from bow to stern against which the steam-bent ribs would be shaped. The steamed oak ribs were through-bolted to the floor timbers to add further strength. Then the planking was laid. It was cedar except for the garboards and sheerstrakes. These, Beaton made of mahogany.

"All the old boats I've worked on," he said, "have the garboard all chewed up, so I wanted a harder wood than cedar. I used mahogany at the sheerstrake because it holds fasteners better and the sheerstrake on these boats carries a lot of load."

As *Wasp* took shape on the wooden floor of the old shop that Pop Beaton had built, word began to leak out to the sailing community. Every so often, someone would arrive to stare in wonder at the many gracefully curved frames and the sturdy keel. The builders ceased to be amazed, after a time, at just how *many* people were profoundly moved at the rebirth of something that was a part of yachting's past as well as their own.

"They would tell us," said Beaton, "that at one time they had owned one of these boats or raced in it. It seems that at one time, just about anybody on the bay had some contact with the A cats."

Beaton's primary worry, as *Wasp* progressed, did not involve the hull at all. He was concerned about bending the big mahogany plank that would become the

In the shop at Beaton's, Wasp nears completion. (Stan Grayson photos)

cabin sides. The board he would use was 16 inches wide and 1½ inches thick. This wood was Amazon mahogany, a species he had little experience with, and he was not certain of its bending properties. Every time he looked at it, he wondered if the big board might just split instead of forming the sweeping curve it would be called upon to adopt. A week before the plank was needed, Beaton took it out and soaked it in the bay. When the time came for its installation, the Amazon mahogany plank presented no problem at all.

"It bent around there just as easy as could be," Lally Beaton said. He began to lay the cedar decks, screwing the planks to the deckbeams. The decks were constructed contrary to the boatbuilding manuals Beaton has seen, for the planks were laid so that the outside of the tree was facing down, rather than up. Beaton has found that planks tend *not* to curl up, when laid this way, as the annual rings try to straighten out.

"So every plank," he said, "was contrary to boatbuilding's bibles. But when the planks are laid according to those books, they curl and all the edges wear through the canvas."

Canvas was used on decks and cabintop because all the other A cats were canvased and because the Beatons are not at all convinced that fiberglass works as well.

"It doesn't last as long as canvas," Beaton said, "and certainly doesn't seem to add much strength."

The canvas was warmed by the shop's woodstove to get out any moisture. Then it was laid atop a thick coat of paint from which the thinner had been poured off. After the canvas was stretched tight, a thin coat of paint was brushed into its surface.

"We use a thin coat on the theory that it merges with the thick base coat," said Beaton. "It seems to make a very sound job."

By the time canvasing was complete, the Beatons had been working on the boat for some 24 months, the work proceeding slowly around the daily chores in the yard. Sometimes there were weeks with no progress at all, but Hartranft never complained.

"He stuck to our agreement perfectly," said Lally Beaton. "We could have built the boat in a year if that were all we worked on. But we have the yard to run."

As *Wasp* at last neared completion, work on the spars and hardware began. No suitable fittings could be found, so patterns were made for the double-banded gooseneck and the rudder fittings. The mast was built right in the shop, 49 feet of hollow strength. It was one of two masts Beaton built for Hartranft, since *Bat*'s mast, spliced two or three times, had finally succumbed 100 yards from the finish of a race after a forestay strap had broken. Hartranft had two masts built at that time, and one of them went right into *Wasp*. The boom was made of a spruce log, sawed in half and scooped out with round planes to reduce its weight.

Early in June 1982, some three years after *Wasp*'s keel was laid, Hartranft mailed launching-party invitations to those he felt would enjoy being present at the first such ceremony in many years. "Messrs. Lachlan Beaton, Nelson Hartranft and Marshel Moorhouse, Jr. request the pleasure of your company at the historical launching of the WASP, Saturday June 19, 1982, 1300 hours," the card read. Hartranft arranged for the band from Brick Township High School to come and play the national anthem as the flag-bedecked catboat was lowered into the water.

On June 19, it rained. Sunday was Father's Day. *Wasp* was lowered into the bay without the high school band, then otherwise engaged, to play the anthem, but the crowd sang it unaccompanied. Hartranft's wife, Marilyn, broke a bottle of champagne on the big bronze fitting that holds the three forestays, and Hartranft had his picture taken standing beside his new boat. He wore a blue blazer and white cap and looked much like those 19th-century yachtsmen one sees in pictures reproduced from old glass-plate negatives. Old-timers, who actually remembered *Tamwock* and had sailed in other A cats in the Thirties, looked at *Wasp* and saw half-forgotten bits of their lives come floating back to them like sails trimmed to a gentle breeze.

"These boats," said one, "just seem to go on and on."

A week later, *Wasp*, with Lally Beaton aboard, sailed her first race. Despite problems with an ill-setting sail, she triumphed. Beaton's initial impression of the boat was that she was just a little more tender than the Mower-designed A cats. Sailmaker Moorhouse went back to work and added longer batten pockets so that the sail's roach would stand up better. This was the third A cat sail he had built.

"We had a sail plan," he said. "Unfortunately, it was for a cotton sail. We followed it, and when we hoisted sail it was a complete disaster because the battens were not long enough. It wasn't too bad going to windward, but running, about a third of the sail was just flapping."

He made the necessary modifications. The overall goal in making the new sails has been to eliminate the sail as a variable by making sure each boat's sail is the equal of the others. "Before *Wasp* came along, the boat that had the latest sail invariably had the edge," Moorhouse said.

He has now equipped, at a modest price, three A cats with new sails, and he plans to make sails for the others, too. "I do it," said Moorhouse, who is a candid and friendly man, "just to do it. When I am old, I want to look back and say I had a part in this rebirth that Nelson Hartranft got going. I'd like to see more boats built and know they'll be here long after I'm gone. Maybe my grandchildren will be sailing one of them someday."

Hartranft's devotion to promoting the A cats, to sharing his lifelong enthusiasm with others, is unrelenting. For the 1983 season, he determined to let *others* skipper his boats. He made only one stipulation—that two of the crew be young people from the Ocean Gate Yacht Club. He himself would sail *Wasp* in only one race, the Toms River Challenge Cup, in an effort to improve on 1982's performance.

The notion that being part of the A cat effort is somehow historically meaningful and possesses an essential worth that goes beyond any selfish motive has occurred to more people than sailmaker Skip Moorhouse. It seems to characterize everybody who has been around the boats. It is as though Nelson Hartranft's boyhood dream of owning an A cat and of perpetuating the class has become the dream of many men.

"His is an unselfish goal, believe me," said Lally Beaton. He was standing next to his big bandsaw, amid a pile of wood shavings that smelled better than fresh-cut grass. Behind him was the empty place that *Wasp* had occupied for the three years

Spy *awaits work at Beaton's. (Stan Grayson photo)*

it took him and his son and their helpers to build her. A cold October rain, flung at the old shop by a northwest wind, rattled on the window panes and puddled up in the mud and sand outside.

Just beyond the windows, looming over several parked cars, was a boat. It was vaguely misshapen, humped just a bit where the backstays attached, a kind of Quasimodo of A cats. Lally Beaton knew what had happened to the boat.

"Sweisguth," he said, "had hanging knees on his boats, but the Mower boats did not, and knees are probably a good thing. They help keep the sheer straight on one of these."

The boat had other problems, too. The skeg had been built in two pieces and was loosening up, and the centerboard trunk leaked badly and needed to be replaced. The boat in the rain was *Spy*. Lally Beaton looked out at her and briefly, thoughtfully, rubbed a finger against the side of his face. Somehow, Nelson Hartranft's dream had become a part of his life, too, and *Spy* was the next installment in an ongoing story. That winter, he would start another project nobody else wanted. He would begin again to bring an old A cat back to life.

6

The Maid

O F ALL THAT BRIGHT panoply of American yacht designers at work during the
years just before the turn of the century and the two or three decades
immediately thereafter, none created a boat of more lasting fame than did William
Gardner. It was Gardner who designed the schooner *Atlantic*, the 185-foot three-
master that sped across the Atlantic in 1905 in 12 days 4 hours, creating a legend
that has lived on ever since.

There is no indication that Gardner ever designed catboats, as did his famous
contemporaries, A. Cary Smith, Nathanael Herreshoff, and Edward Burgess. But
one of Gardner's most accomplished disciples did. He took what he had learned
from the man he revered as "one of the leading naval architects of the world" and
designed catboats as well as yachts of many other types. This man was Francis
Sweisguth. Born in Union City, New Jersey, in 1882, a graduate of Cooper Union and
the Pratt Institute, Sweisguth never achieved the legendary status of his great
mentor. He was a quiet, private man who did nothing to attract attention to himself
but design good boats. One of the few articles he ever wrote was not about a design
of his own, but about Gardner. He worked at Gardner's office at One Broadway,
New York City, for some 20 years, and he might even have helped with the drafting
of *Atlantic*. But by the early to mid-1920s, when Gardner withdrew from yacht
design, eyes ruined by too many nights at candlelit drawing boards, Sweisguth was
employed as a naval architect in City Island in a firm that came to be known as
Ford, Payne and Sweisguth.

Neither of his colleagues in this enterprise ever learned much more about

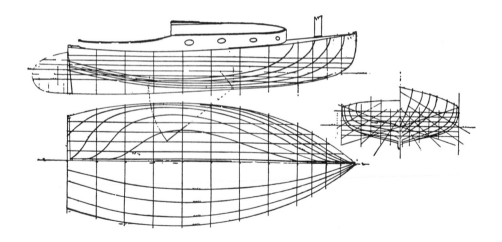

The lines of the 30-foot Sweisguth catboat Scat II. (Sailing Craft, *edited by Edwin J. Schoettle)*

Sweisguth than that he shared Gardner's love for classical music—both Sweisguth and his wife were pianists—and that he kept very much to himself.

"He was," said Gerald Ford, "very reserved and quiet. Gardner was a quiet fellow, too, but Sweisguth was so close-mouthed as to be gloomy."

Ford believed that Sweisguth developed an interest in catboats when he lived in Point Pleasant, New Jersey, and that he did a number of catboat designs for Philadelphians who summered at the Jersey shore. One of these Philadelphians was Edwin Schoettle. When he was 24 years old in 1900, Schoettle acquired a powerful Wilton Crosby–built racing catboat he called *Scat*, the boat built originally for racing enthusiast Frank Randall in 1896.

Schoettle took *Scat* to Barnegat Bay, where he raced and cruised aboard her for 20 years before he decided it was time to build a new boat. This was a 30-footer with a 12-foot beam, and he named her *Scat II*. Designed by Sweisguth, she was built in Berkeley, near Seaside Park, by the Townsend Boatyard, and won the Bay Championship during her first year out in 1921. This performance so enthused one of Schoettle's friends that he commissioned Charles Mower to design the first of what became the A cats, prompting development of boats even faster than *Scat II*. When that happened, Schoettle went right back to Sweisguth and asked for a boat that would go better than the mighty As. The result became one of the most famous craft ever to sail Barnegat Bay. Schoettle called her *Silent Maid*.

"The *Scat II*'s lines were drawn and redrawn until the correct curve of areas was obtained," Schoettle wrote years later in the book he entitled *Sailing Craft*, "and great care was necessarily taken to obtain just the desired shape of waterline forward.... In designing *Silent Maid*, it was decided to keep about the same waterline length [*Scat II*'s was 28 feet], but about six inches were added to the forward overhang and, instead of the conventional square stern, she was given an overhang of 2 feet, 4 inches. The same fine waterline forward was retained. The extra overall length permitted the waterline aft to be sharpened, thus improving the reaching and running qualities. This extra overall length, especially forward,

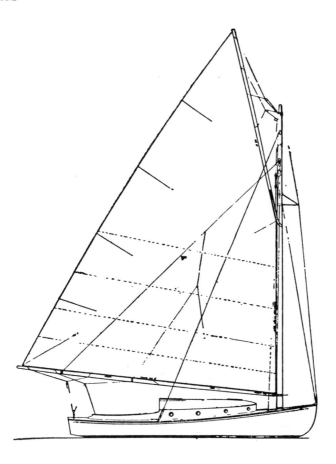

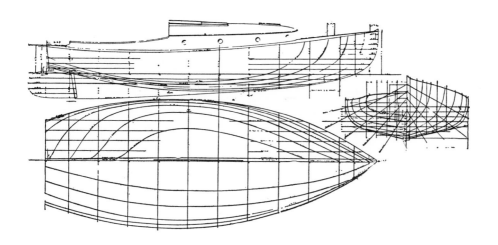

The sail plan and lines of Silent Maid *(Sailing Craft, edited by Edwin J. Schoettle)*

provided a better and longer list line, more power for windward work, and also eased the helm when off the wind. In a strong breeze the long low overhangs and the extra length gained by heeling, as the *Silent Maid* uses practically all her length when heeled, gives her the power to carry the sail and to go in a breeze much faster than the conventional square stern cat."

With *Silent Maid*, Sweisguth had created a particularly well-balanced catboat that carried 950 square feet of sail on a 33-foot overall length, a 28-foot 6-inch waterline, and a reasonably narrow 12-foot 6-inch beam. Draft, board up, was 2 feet 6 inches, permitting the boat to be sailed over much of shallow Barnegat Bay. Schoettle said that Sweisguth, in designing this boat, "made an exhaustive search of details concerning all famous boats known to have possessed more than the ordinary amount of merit. The *Silent Maid* is the composite result of this work." In fact, the boat's overall shape resembled nothing so much as Sweisguth's earlier, smaller catboats.

Silent Maid was built to a very high standard at Morton Johnson's yard in Bay Head. No engine was installed—hence the boat's name—for Schoettle much preferred to do without power. He delighted in nothing so much as the chance to tow home a disabled motorboat. *Silent Maid*'s topsides were finished bright. She was fastened together with precision and strength. The chainplates were reinforced with bronze straps. Lead was fitted flush into the bottom of the wooden keel and additional ballast was added inside as formed lead sheets molded over the frames. To Schoettle, *Silent Maid* was the boat of a lifetime. He won five class championships beginning in 1925, eventually acquiring such a substantial time penalty that it took much of the fun out of racing. But Schoettle enjoyed sailing for its own sake. 'We'd all go sailing," his daughter Mary remembered, "my friends, mother and father. Whenever we'd have guests for the weekend, Father would just love to take them sailing and have interesting conversations out there on the bay."

Each year, Schoettle and his family cruised the big catboat down the bay, past the barrier islands that are now covered with housing but were then wild and beautiful places of grass and wind-beaten trees and long, white beaches. He used her thus for some 23 years while keeping active his fascination with sailboats of all types. Nowhere was this interest more evident than in the book he edited for the Macmillan Company in 1928. *Sailing Craft* is a compendium of pieces covering everything from Stars to New York Forties, sail design, schooners, Barnegat Bay sneakboxes, and a New York-to-Maine cruise described by Cornelius Vanderbilt, Jr. It was an all-encompassing look at American yachting such as has seldom been published before or since. Schoettle wrote several chapters himself, including one called "American Catboats" that featured, needless to say, *Silent Maid*.

After Schoettle died in 1947, *Silent Maid* was sold to Blakely and Frances Chandley of Bay Head, the first of several subsequent owners. Somewhat daunted by the large sail, they reduced its size slightly, and promptly installed a Gray four-cylinder engine, thus rendering "the *Maid*," as she was known to sailors in Barnegat Bay, rather less silent than before. "They just couldn't imagine," said Schoettle's daughter, "how Mother and Father managed to sail it themselves, because they, years younger, wouldn't have dared sail it without power and more crew." The Chandleys sold the *Maid* to James and Betty Kellogg, who had previously bought both *Scat* and *Lotus* from Schoettle and had even sailed *Scat* to

Maine. In the mid-1960s, the Kelloggs sold. "We only kept *Silent Maid* for a couple of years," said Betty Kellogg. "She was just too much for us." The new owner delighted in sailing out through Manasquan Inlet with some 20 people in the cockpit, anchoring off the beach, and having an enormous waterborne party. By the time he decided to sell after only a couple of years of ownership, the *Maid*'s status was well-established—a legend, in fact. When a driver education teacher named Sally Schneider saw a listing for the boat tacked to a broker's bulletin board, she came to an immediate and, for her, startling conclusion.

"I said to myself," she remembered, "I *have* to own her."

She had a fiberglass Columbia Challenger she was tired of, and the idea of owning the big old catboat was born in her like one of those cartoon lightbulbs that is switched on with a distinct CLICK. "Every broker at the Shore had the *Maid* listed," Schneider said, "but nobody seemed to know where she was at a given time. I figured, OK, I'm going to find her."

She drove up and down the Jersey shore, looking in at each and every marina. One gray day, she was driving across the bridge at Manasquan and happened to look down. "I saw," she said, "this big, tall mast." She managed to find out where the owner lived and called him on the telephone. He said he was selling the *Maid* because he wanted a boat with a shower. "We had a very short discussion," Schneider said, "and I told him, 'Well, let me go to the credit union.' I went there and showed them the picture of the boat in Schoettle's book. I said, 'I *want* this.' They were flabbergasted. Five thousand dollars was a lot of money in 1967 or 1968."

Schneider had a survey performed, and then, in January 1968, she fulfilled her dream and became the fifth owner of *Silent Maid*, or, perhaps, the fifth person owned *by Silent Maid*. She decided that during the first year of this mutual ownership she would try to do as much sailing as possible. The major question raised by survey was the condition of the garboard planks, but Schneider believed repairs there could wait, as could the tired centerboard trunk.

"I knew I wanted to sail her," she said, "but, of course, I didn't really know *how* to sail her. I looked at the rigging and didn't know what anything meant. Two old salts at Beaton's trained me."

She sailed the old boat hard. She went out in heavy winds. The boat leaked and it took two bilge pumps to keep her going. The treelike mast seemed to open the boat up in hard going, and the seams would not close again until the boat again lay still in her slip. The leaks restricted *Silent Maid*'s cruising range. One night, at anchor with two friends, their four children, and a dog, Schneider awoke to find the dog climbing into her berth.

"I couldn't understand that," she said. "Then I realized the dog had wet feet. We were *sinking* right there in the middle of Barnegat Bay, at anchor, at night. It took us five hours to pump her out."

After that first season of sailing, the leaks and other problems forced Schneider to begin a comprehensive maintenance program that has continued ever since. The varnish began peeling off, and the sail—her original cotton sail, which only a crew of 10 people or more could heft—needed numerous patches. The loose rudderpost was beefed up and the entire boat was painted. With those tasks complete, Schneider began remodeling the cabin, restoring it from the compartmentalized, Formica-surfaced place it had become to the open arrangement Sweisguth had intended. She decided not to rebuild the centerboard, which had been cut down at some point, making the cabin roomier—although not roomy enough for a shower—but decreasing the boat's windward ability.

The boat required endless care. It was hard to keep up with the paint and varnish demands. Schneider listened in awe one day to an old-timer who happened by the yard, recognized the *Maid*, and told how he had maintained her once-varnished hull and cabin for a time when, as a boy, Schoettle had hired him. But Schneider had nobody but herself and friends who did not have boats of their own. She kept *Silent Maid* at Beaton's in a slip next to the little houseboat she inhabited during the summer for a number of years and battled to keep the catboat going. Friends helped whenever they could, and Ken Mapes, who was then developing his special artistry at restoration, commiserated with her during work breaks from his own catboat and advised her about new maintenance techniques he had learned.

Gradually, as years passed, the *Maid* became a way of life for Sally Schneider, and she formed a sort of love-hate relationship with the boat. She began looking at her, lying low and long in the slip, and asking herself, "What *next*?" Sometimes, she felt overwhelmed when her love faltered. Once she offered the *Maid* for sale in *The New York Times*.

"I was afraid I was losing it," she said. "Owning this boat is like a trust, an obligation to the past. I began to feel as if I might not be able to keep faith with it, as if I just could not afford it."

People responded to the ad and came to look at the boat. Many of them seemed to be doctors or lawyers from Connecticut. One offered to trade her a painting that was hanging then in the Museum of Modern Art. Schneider said she loved art but that only a Wyeth would be of interest to her. Her desire to sell the boat began to waver. Another prospective buyer came down to inspect the *Maid*, and when he had looked her over, he returned with $17,000 and laid out all the bills on the dropleaf table in the cabin.

"That was serious," said Schneider. "It was in *piles*. I said, 'You can't buy her that way. You have to have a survey. We can't have anything hidden.'"

The man paid for the survey. Again, it pointed out a need for new garboards in addition to some other problems. The buyer reduced his offer to $10,000, giving Schneider the excuse she did not know she'd been looking for. "I was never so glad to see a boat fail a survey," she said. "He told me that maybe he'd put a bowsprit on the boat and do some other things. I was getting totally panicked."

She did not respond to the $10,000 offer. Instead, she renewed her commitment to the *Maid*. She hired an expert old caulker, a native of the Jersey Pine Barrens who had worked once at Johnson Brothers. Deftly, the old man did his work, his caulking mallet tapping out a metallic symphony as it drove an ever-changing thickness of cotton into the seams. He did a good job but, when he was finished, the boat still leaked at the garboards. After that, Schneider went to see Lally Beaton and convinced him to find the time to install new garboard planks in *Silent Maid*.

In the fall of 1981, *Silent Maid* was hauled for major surgery. Sally and friends went to work to remove the old garboards. "We had all these drills with hole cutters," she said, "and it took four of us four weekends to get the planks off. Lally told us to try to get them off in one piece to preserve them as patterns. It was really

Sally Schneider at the helm of Silent Maid *(Stan Grayson photo)*

hard. They're a little over an inch thick. It was so difficult I can't even explain it. They might have leaked but they were tightly fastened. We found nails in there; we found screws. It went on and on."

When the old planks were finally off, Lally Beaton told Schneider he wanted to move the boat closer to his shop. She couldn't face the prospect of being present during this delicate operation. She went to Cape Cod. When she returned, the *Maid* was sitting beside Beaton's door and there were jacks all around her and chains and straps rigged everywhere. Schneider had owned the boat for so long, seeing her so often, that she never noticed the *Maid* had, like some once-young, lithe woman, grown droopy with age. Now the old boat was being racked by the straps and chains and jacks as if undergoing some sort of boatyard inquisition. As the Beatons tightened up on these devices, plugs began popping out of fastener holes and the boat regained its proper sheer. Wedges were driven in between the frames and keel to replace the ones that had rotted and fallen out. At last, new garboards were installed. Tommy Beaton said the job was straightforward.

"We used the old ones as spiling battens," he said. "There's a little twist up forward but nothing difficult."

With the new garboards installed, the *Maid* was returned to her slip beside the houseboat and the Marshall Sanderling that Schneider campaigns with great success together with her friend Marie Darling. The *Maid* spent the winter of 1981-

Silent Maid is a friendly boat and there's always room for more crew. (Stan Grayson photo)

82 in wet storage while Schneider looked ahead to spring. Then she planned to undertake the next big job on her never-ending maintenance list.

"This whole thing," she said, "is an expensive, long-term *disease*."

Because curing the *Maid*'s diseases has proved an ongoing and time-consuming business, the season was well advanced before the boat was ready for a demonstration sail. But, on a sunny afternoon in late June, with a crew of nine aboard, we slipped the mooring lines for a gentle romp in the gray-brown waters just south of Mantoloking. The engine, an Atomic Four that had replaced the original Gray, started quick as a tick, and we headed out of Beaton's placid lagoon. As soon as we reached open water, the sail gaskets were removed by various crewmembers stationed here and there along the boom.

On *Silent Maid*, the throat halyard belays to port, the peak halyard, to starboard. Tom Fitzpatrick began heaving on the throat halyard while I tailed. Our actions were duplicated on the peak by Marie Darling's son Eddie and by Charley Best, who owns an unusual Ray Hunt–designed double-ender that he berths near *Silent Maid*. Schneider said that when she bought the boat, one person could raise and lower the sail fairly easily. Then one day an old-timer said, "Well, Sal, let's take everything off the mast and replace all the rigging." But they failed to make diagrams before they did so, and when they rerigged the boat, the purchase was somehow wrong and it took at least two people to hoist sail. Schneider is still working on this problem and believes it will soon be solved with the discovery of Sweisguth's original sail plan in the collection of the Suffolk Marine Museum on Long Island.

With four willing hands on the halyards, the big sail quickly ascended the mast, a hollow, brightly varnished spar some 47 feet tall. It is a splendid thing, supported by shrouds and running backstays, and it presents enough windage so that Schneider once ran under a bare pole for several miles in a rather light breeze, just for fun. "My, you have a quiet engine," marveled a curious passing sailor. Once the halyards were neatly coiled, we beat our way past a miniature forest of saplings, newly embedded in the muddy bottom to mark some clam beds.

"They're just starting to transfer harvested clams here for holding while the clams purge themselves of contamination," said Charley Best, "but they've taken away a lot of water." The saplings quivered slightly in the southerly breeze that we judged to be some 12 knots.

In that wind, *Silent Maid* handled easily, showing weather helm only in the occasional puffs. It seemed a long way from the helmsman's perch to the bow, but the view over the broad, low cabintop was one of grandeur. We slipped along to windward, with Schneider pointing out the new sail panels sewn in by Marie Darling. The entire sail exhibits fine handwork, the cringles and boltrope beautifully executed by a friend of Schneider's whom she describes as "an old English gentleman who worked on oil tankers."

The sail set nicely and we eased along in a manner that can only be described as majestic. Charley Best and his girlfriend Jan passed up a box full of fresh sandwiches from the cabin and soon everyone was eating, talking, and waving to those who waved at us. "*Silent Maid!*" some of them called.

"This boat," said Charley Best, "is an institution on the bay."

Once, Jimmy Kellogg, a former owner of *Silent Maid*, was visiting South Africa, and there, in Durban, discovered of all things a catboat under construction. He began talking with one of the boatwrights and said, "It might interest you to know that I have sailed in one of the fastest catboats ever built."

The boatwright did not even hesitate. "I bet you're talking about the *Silent Maid*," he said. "I helped build her a long time ago in Bay Head."

We reached and ran the afternoon away until finally, in the waters off Beaton's again, we started the engine and rounded into the wind. The sail came down smoothly and was quickly furled. A few minutes later, we were tied up in the slip eating fresh fruit and giving some thanks that the wind, now gusting to more than 20 knots, had spared us. Schneider has sailed the boat reefed, when necessary, in winds gusting to 30 or better, but she has found the *Maid* to be a handful in those conditions and unwilling to tack readily, perhaps because of the cut-down centerboard. But now, we could sit comfortably and talk while friends of Schneider's dropped by to ask how the boat was shaping up. *Silent Maid* remains a kind of social focal point at Beaton's, a happy boat that attracts attention from all sorts of people. As we talked, visitors stopped by to say hello and stand with hands on hips looking up at the mast, which had been stepped only a few days earlier with the aid of a crane mounted on a 100-foot barge.

"It's just too much for the yard crane to handle," said Schneider of the *Maid*'s mast, "but it was a little embarrassing to have that enormous barge come in here."

Silent Maid *reaching easily across Barnegat Bay during the summer of 1983. The big sail plan requires a mast supported by shrouds and running back-stays. (Stan Grayson photo)*

Silent Maid was due to be hauled shortly. She was to be freshly painted and to have her leaky rudder tube, a problem she shares with the old A cats, replaced. Schneider looked forward to this particular repair with special anticipation, since it promised her a really dry bilge for the first time. She also planned some additional varnishing.

"Will that about take care of things?" I asked.

"It would," she answered, "except there are those cabin leaks and that's why I'm going to recanvas the whole top of the cabin."

"You mean take off all the rails and moldings and fittings?"

She looked over at the cabintop. "It's all got to come off," she said, "and so does the fiberglass that was put on at some point instead of canvas. But when we're done, she'll be dry bottom *and* top."

The extent of the work before her did not seem to bother Sally Schneider. For a long time now, her relationship with the *Maid* had been on a love cycle, rolling smoothly like a gentle, deep-green ground swell undulating toward some white, sandy beach.

"Sometimes, if I get down about the work," she said, "I think about what the man I bought her from said one summer as we sailed by."

"What was that?" I asked.

"He was aboard his 65-foot yawl," Schneider answered. "He yelled over at us. At first I couldn't understand what he was saying, so I cupped my hand over my ear and he said it again. What he shouted was this: 'Why did I ever sell her for a shower?'"

7

"More Open than Usual"

A SWORDFISH, WHEN IT FEEDS, searches out a school of mackerel, herring, or other fish, and attacks with its sword. It slashes from side to side, killing its prey and eating its fill. Then, contented, the swordfish basks peacefully near the surface. The remains of its meal—bits of fish and fish oil—emit a peculiar scent, much like the smell of watermelon, and that is sometimes the first thing a fisherman notices as he seeks his prey. Other times, a lookout at the masthead will spot the swordfish swimming along, a reddish-blue shape 10 or 15 feet beneath the surface, or perhaps shallower, showing a fin or tail now and then.

Old fishermen from Cape Cod and the islands remember the 1920s as a kind of high point in the swordfishery. At the end of May, they readied their harpoons and lines and prepared to go out after the swordfish swimming in Nantucket Sound and in the waters around Block Island. Fleets of schooners from Gloucester, New Bedford, and Maine went after swordfish, too, and fishermen in the larger boats would follow the fish to Georges Banks. Southwest from Nomans Land was good also. That was where mackerel could be netted in spring, swordfish taken in summer, and cod in the fall.

Versatile as they were, catboats were often used for swordfishing. Charlie Sayle, who began fishing from Nantucket in 1930, remembers quite a few catboats in the fishery. Although some were rigged as sloops, others retained the single sail. All were fitted with one-lunger engines, and most were comparatively large, 30 to 32 feet. Larger vessels were required because swordfish are large creatures and because the fishermen often had to go well out to sea to pursue them.

An anonymous photographer found a worthy subject in this catboat named Gem, *docked at New Bedford in 1918. With her mast stepped through the cabintop,* Gem *could set a small jib. The addition of chainplates and shrouds suggests she might have been used for dragging, and the neatly folded net in her cockpit carries cork floats and was used for mackerel seining. (Courtesy The Whaling Museum, New Bedford, Massachusetts)*

The last such vessel that Sayle remembers seeing was *Clara T.*, a 42-foot sloop-rigged catboat that belonged to a fisherman named Bob Sanchez. "He gave me a mess of fish and we had quite a talk," said Sayle, "and the following fall he was lost off Nomans. That was about 1955 or so."

Although a schooner with an ice-filled hold could stay out for some weeks if necessary, most of the catboatmen who went after swordfish stayed out no longer than a day or two. These catboats were fitted with long, wide bowsprits, at the end of which a pulpit was mounted. There the fisherman would stand, dressed as often as not in a vest and dapper hat, his harpoon in his hands. Frequently, a ladder was rigged to the forward side of the mast, and a lookout, posted at the masthead, would scout for fish and sing out promptly if he spotted one. A block and tackle rigged to the mast could be used to haul up the swordfish by the tail. Then the fish could be carried home, mouth agape, on the deck or cabintop, safe from the jaws of sharks.

Once the fish had been "ironed," a keg was tossed overboard. It was attached to the end of the harpoon's line and acted as a drag to tire the fish. The catboats towed a dory or two, and a crewman would go out in the dory and fetch the keg, playing the fish as best he could. It was tricky work; occasionally, a fish would go for the dory and attack.

"One fella here," said Charlie Sayle, "got stabbed about the legs, got his legs ripped up. When you saw one coming, what you did, why you'd get up on the thwarts. They could get real mean."

The days when catboats could be seen cruising for swordfish, their big sails set and drawing and a sharp-eyed boy seated at the masthead, are long over. The vessels themselves have long since disappeared. Some burned up when the fuel lines supplying their single-cylinder make-and-break engines broke, and the volatile gasoline caught fire. A few were lost to the same summer gales that sank larger vessels. Others were condemned after working careers that spanned a quarter-century or more, succumbing, in the end, to the ravages of wood rot, time, and hard use.

There are not many photographs depicting the fishery as it was. One shows a brawny-looking 30-footer tied up in Menemsha, on Martha's Vineyard, sometime around 1920. This big catboat was named *Beatrice*, and she was built in Wareham, Massachusetts, by Charles Anderson. I saw her ghost one day 60 years later. It was sitting on a mooring in Winthrop Harbor, not far from the busy runways of Logan Airport.

The old boatbuilder sat in front of a fireplace in which one enormous log burned slowly. It was February, and there was but a single shaft of sunlight filtering into the dusty office. The man's dog slept on the one chair warmed by the sun.

"I did my best," the boatbuilder remembered, "to help the old fella. I used to let him launch his boats down here, put 'em on my railway. If he had a boat to rebuild, I'd let him haul it on my railway and he and the two boys would work on it there."

That is what Lester Goodwin, owner of Cape Cod Shipbuilding, remembered of his dealings with Charles Anderson. He first met him in 1939 when Anderson was 69 years old. A year earlier, Anderson's big shop in Wareham had been destroyed by the great hurricane. On the day after the storm, a friend saw Anderson standing amid the wreckage of his boatyard. "Are you open for business?" he asked.

Anderson looked around him at stacks of wood, collapsed walls, and a profusion of cedar shingles. "More open than usual," he answered in his singsong English.

Charles A. Anderson was born in Sweden in 1870. He came to the United States with his parents nine years later, and the family settled in Wareham. At the age of 14, when Anderson refused to attend school any longer, he got a job as a water carrier in an iron foundry. He stayed at the foundry until he was 18 and then took a job in an East Boston shipyard, where he remained for two years. When he returned home, he began building skiffs, and soon, larger boats. When he had no work, he drove to Providence in a Chalmers car he had bought and worked for boatbuilders there. But apparently, by the end of World War I, Charles Anderson had enough work to keep himself busy on a fairly steady basis.

"When he'd get an order or two for a boat, he'd build a catboat," said a Wareham native who knew Anderson.

But Anderson built boats of all sorts in the shop he set up at the Narrows Bridge on the Wareham River. He built *Alert*, the ferry that still runs from New Bedford to Cuttyhunk. He built *Nor'easter*, a 57-foot motorsailer for Henry DuPont; sloops; and fishing boats. The biggest boat he built was 268 feet long; the smallest were his

Swordfishing under sail. **Above:** Natalie, *a cat-hulled, sloop-rigged vessel of about 42 feet, has a lookout posted at her masthead while the harpooner waits in the pulpit.* **Right:** *The harpooner sends his dart, and the fish is struck.* **Opposite top:** Natalie's *fishermen haul in their prey. Note the kegs used to tire the fish after they've been struck, and the lack of cockpit seats.* **Bottom:** *Landed! (A.C. Church photos. Courtesy The Whaling Museum, New Bedford, Massachusetts)*

Beatrice, *a Charles Anderson catboat. (Courtesy John Leavens)*

skiffs and daysailing catboats. All these vessels were built heavily. Routinely, Anderson used larger stock than plans called for.

"He was," said Lester Goodwin, "an honest workman, as honest as the day is long. The boats were better built, with better joinerwork. For the money, though, I'm not sure they were actually better. I sometimes thought they were so heavy they might defeat their purpose."

Because no commercial hardware was heavy enough to suit Anderson, he made his own. He was also fussy about the engines he installed and was critical of them all. He used Palmers and Mianus two-cycles and, later, Gray four-cycles. Whether or not Anderson designed every boat he built is unknown. He did work from plans—although no catboat plans seem to have survived—and half-models. Early in the century he built a number of decked, daysailing catboats, and later, much larger catboats. There is nothing to indicate that Anderson's larger catboats were intended primarily for fishing rather than pleasure sailing, but the sheer size of one of his 30-footers made them suitable for such work.

Most of Anderson's boats possessed a pronounced sheer, greater than that of a typical Crosby, and the larger boats seem to have had underhung rather than barndoor rudders. The two surviving 30-footers possess double companionways and standing headroom. The boats were usually ballasted with pig iron and fastened with galvanized iron nails made nearby at the old Tremont Nail Works. Cedar planks and oak frames characterize Anderson's boats, although he sometimes used cypress, too.

Charles Anderson was a gifted craftsman. He was famous among boatbuilders who knew him for a machine he invented to mass-produce plugs for fastener holes. When the town of Wareham needed someone to design a water main to pipe water across the Wareham River, Anderson did the job, and it was Anderson, rather than a trained engineer, who repaired the Narrows Bridge. When he wasn't working on

Charles Anderson's boatshop, Wareham, circa 1930. (Courtesy John Freeburg)

boats or civil engineering projects, he diverted himself by making violins and banjos. None of this activity seems to have earned him a particularly comfortable living, however. After the 1938 hurricane, Anderson rebuilt his boatyard, but nobody today recalls the new yard as being anything like the first. It was smaller, for one thing, and six years after it was built, it too was destroyed in the hurricane of 1944.

"He got tired of regenerating after hurricanes," said Goodwin, "so he sold the land down there and got no money and moved his shop up the hill."

The new shop was located next to Anderson's old house in Wareham. Anderson worked there until 1953, when he fell from a boat and later died in the hospital after an unsuccessful operation. Lester Goodwin thought it would be interesting to see the place, and we drove up for a look. When we got there, however, Goodwin pulled off the road, puzzled. The house was still there but the shop was gone. Instead, there was only an empty field of red dirt. Later, we learned the shop had been burned to the ground by vandals.

"I wonder," said Goodwin, "what became of that great old plug-cutting machine?"

The Anderson catboat in Winthrop was named *Sea Cat*. Built sometime in the 1920s, she was now owned by Arthur Cotta, a longtime catboat enthusiast who kept her on a mooring he could see from his living room window. To Cotta, the part of Winthrop Harbor where his boat lay was "Cat Cove." *Sea Cat* replaced Cotta's first catboat, a Crosby 21-footer, after he married. His wife, Gladys, was a schoolteacher and would have summers free for cruising. Cotta began making ambitious plans, looking forward to sailing in comfort along the New England coast. He was willing to invest heavily in such a future. When he discovered *Sea Cat*, she was named *Tom* and was in rough shape, and she needed extensive modifications before she would suit his plans. But her dilapidated condition only stirred a vision in him. He made plans for a new cabin with counters, a galley, a Shipmate stove, and an icebox.

"I figured I'd have two lowers and two upper berths with backs that would swing down for sitting," he said. "Then there would be a door to the forepeak and a sink and a head. So that's what I did." He paused, reconsidering a time almost 25 years before. "Well," he said, "I had ideas and dreams."

When Cotta bought his big catboat in the early 1960s, he thought she had been built by the Crosbys, since that is what her previous owners told him. However, when he made a trip to Osterville to look through such plans as survived and to talk with the Crosby family, he learned nothing to indicate that his new boat had indeed been built there. He began to wonder if she might have been built by Manuel Swartz Roberts or by C.C. Hanley. But nobody seemed to know. Wishing he knew more, Cotta began working on the boat, which still lay in the Marshfield yard where he had found her.

He rolled up his sleeves and went to work removing ballast so that he could clean the bilge. The ballast was in lead bars, 2,000 pounds of them. Each piece was covered with sand, mud, and oil. He took the ballast home to Winthrop in his 1959 Mercury, making four or five trips and breaking two springs in the process. That November, he arranged to have the boat trucked from the Cohasset yard where he had bought her to a yard nearer home, in the marsh at Revere. He cleaned out the bilge and went to work on the topsides, sanding down the planks, which, he found, were made of cedar and fastened to the oak frames with iron boatnails. The nails were driven straight into the frames but not clenched, which pleased him.

"Once you drive an old-fashioned boatnail into oak," he said, "you can't pull it out. And if it's not clenched, the galvanizing isn't ever broken. I thought to myself that *whoever* had built this boat knew what he was doing."

The boat had a deck made of strip-planked pine. The deck leaked. With the help of a man who worked at the Charlestown Navy Yard and had some experience with fiberglass, which was then still a rather new material to most people, Cotta prepared the decks to be fiberglass covered. He removed the toerails, rubrails, and cabintop handrails. An adze was used to cut down the red oak covering board that skirted the decks. Then the deck was planed flat, refastened, and covered with ⅜-inch plywood fastened with bronze nails. The plywood was covered with a layer of fiberglass cloth and two layers of resin. All this came out so well that Cotta, working alone, fiberglassed the cabin sides and cockpit sole, then covered the cabintop with strips of cloth 60 inches wide.

While the fiberglassing was underway, Cotta journeyed around Boston's North and South shores, looking for useful parts and seeking information. One day, he stopped in at the Manchester yard owned by yacht designer Samuel Crocker and told Sam about his boat.

"He asked me what the numbers were and I told him. Then he asked me what the name was. I laughed and said I had changed the name but the boat had been named *Tom*."

Crocker thought for a moment and then said, "*Tom*? Is that the *Tom* that was moored in Scituate Harbor?"

Cotta told him it was, and that he thought, but wasn't sure, the boat had been built by a Crosby. "Oh, no," said Sam Crocker, "that's not a Crosby boat."

Cotta still remembers the sinking feeling he got. "I thought, 'Oh, God!' Because I always thought the best catboat was a Crosby."

But there was Crocker shaking his head. "That is *not* a Crosby boat," he said.

"Look at it this way," Cotta said hopefully, "is it a good boat made by good people?"

Crocker nodded. "That boat," he answered, "is a Charles Anderson boat made down in Wareham. He was a very fussy old Swede who built some of the finest yachts you could imagine."

Later that same week, Fenwick Williams noticed the boat as he rode the train from Marblehead to Boston. He returned to inspect *Sea Cat*, told Cotta how impressed he was by what he was doing, and confirmed that the vessel was one of Anderson's.

"Gee," Cotta said, "I felt lightened when I heard that."

With *Sea Cat*'s decks, cabintop, and cockpit sole completed, Cotta removed the Chrysler Crown Six and replaced it with a 60 horsepower Palmer. Then he began work on the interior. By the time he had bought the boat, the cabin had been divided into two sections. These he ripped out completely. Then he sat in the gutted cabin and began working out what he wanted to do. To help him with his plans, he hired an expert joiner who worked during the day at Ted Hood's yard in Marblehead. Cotta remembers him as being "very, very good and very, very slow. He was amazed at the ideas I had."

Cotta stripped and sanded the entire cabin, which was sheathed with red oak, the staves having been joined by splines rather than tongue and groove, which Arthur claims would have been cheaper. He installed counters and a galley, a chart area, drawers, bins, lockers, and bulkheads. He designed a new dropleaf table, and the man from Hood's built it for him.

"It's too bad I couldn't hang on to him," said Cotta, "because my boat would have been finished the way I wanted it rather than in dribs and drabs. I *still* have to make new cockpit seats!"

He had undertaken an enormous project. Worse, he had begun it at the same time he was remodeling his house. There was not enough time for both, and work on the boat inevitably slowed. "I was," he said, "no spring chicken." He used to sit in the cabin, when he got tired, and dream of cruising.

With the cabin mostly complete, Cotta began working on *Sea Cat*'s rig. When he bought the boat, he learned that the thing its owners had liked least was raising and lowering the sail. They also complained of "loose" steering. Cotta found the babbitt bearing for the steering shaft was worn. He took the shaft to a local machine shop but the owner declined the job. He began a search for a machine shop willing to do the project and finally found one in Gloucester. Then he removed the entire steering gear and took it there. The shop foreman was impressed with the steering system Charles Anderson had built.

"If you ever need to replace *that*," he told Cotta, "it will cost you $250 for the worm gear alone."

The Anderson catboat Sea Cat, *1982. (Stan Grayson photo)*

Cotta next stripped down the boat's great solid mast. Before remounting overhauled blocks, he fabricated steel plates to act as bearing surfaces for the eyebolts that would hold the blocks. That way, the bolts would not sink into the soft spruce mast, break through the varnish, and allow water to enter and begin to rot the wood.

Sea Cat's gaff had obviously been cut down at some time, and Cotta ordered a longer one at the same time he decided to have a new sail made. He began visiting different lofts and searching for more of the bronze slides the boat was missing, since *Sea Cat*'s sail was attached to the mast not by hoops but by slides riding on a bronze track. Here and there, he added to his collection of sail slides, but he found that selecting a sailmaker was difficult.

"These young fellas in their 20s and 30s," he said of the staff of a loft world-famous for its sails, "what did they know about a gaff sail!" He wound up at Smith

Yacht Sails, a traditional loft in Fairhaven, and found a sailmaker who spoke his language. The sailmaker told him to set the boat up so that the boom was horizontal, raise the gaff as high as he wanted the luff to be, measure the length of the gaff, and provide a measurement for the throat down to the clew.

"I gave him the measurements," said Cotta, "and he went right ahead and said not to worry about anything."

When the 585-square-foot sail was finished, Cotta spent an entire afternoon on his mooring, raising the sail to see how it set, lowering it, tying in one or another set of reef points, and raising it again. The sail set perfectly. It was a long afternoon. "I should have called the boat *All Alone*," he said, "because everything I did, I did myself."

It was a cool, sunny afternoon in mid-autumn when Arthur Cotta rowed us in his skiff out to where *Sea Cat* was moored. In a harbor full of motorboats and more modern sailing craft, the big catboat with her bow pulpit and with a ladder leading to her masthead looked exactly like what she was, a reincarnation. There hadn't been a boat like her built in a half century, yet there she was, shimmering in the colors Cotta had selected—white topsides, aqua decks and cabintop, and yellow rubrail. Two red electric horns were mounted on the cabintop.

Cotta had issued repeated warnings about the work involved in preparing *Sea Cat* for an afternoon sail and putting her to bed again afterward. He did not exaggerate. Climbing aboard this eight-ton vessel, I began to think that the word *catship* was more appropriate than *catboat*. The cockpit was a *vast* expanse of aqua paint. Overhead, the boom could have served a schooner twice *Sea Cat's* size. The bulkhead was dominated by the two separate companionways, while, atop the cabin, a big and gracious-looking skylight was mounted.

We removed the sail cover, a job that entailed detaching the peak halyard from its block on the gaff's wire bail. The block was made of bronze, the shells having a pleasing open-grille design. We removed some of the sail gaskets and Cotta stowed them and the sail cover below. Then he removed a canvas cover he keeps over the big Palmer gasoline engine. He bought this engine in 1962, after first inspecting a Red Wing and a Universal. The engine looked beautifully cared for, its gray-green paint still shiny. It turns an 18 by 14, three-bladed propeller.

Sea Cat's cabin is a spacious place, and one can walk about with ease. Cotta, however, was soon on his knees, lifting a floorboard and noting that there was water in the bilge. He had had the garboards replaced, but the job had not been done to his demanding standards, and, occasionally, he still had to pump the boat out.

It was some 40 minutes before we were ready to leave the mooring. We powered slowly out of the harbor, into the teeth of some substantial gusts. A little West Wight Potter was pottering out just ahead of us. We talked briefly of reefing, something Cotta has never done with the boat underway. He does tie in a single reef if the wind seems to blow a steady 18 knots, but he does so before leaving the mooring. This day, he said we'd go with full sail. We turned out of the harbor along a stone seawall, the gusts still coming strong. The Potter had lost a shroud; its mast had come down and the boat was pulled up on a beach. As we neared the open water of Boston Harbor, however, the gusts suddenly diminished in strength and frequency, and by the time I moved forward to raise sail, there was barely any wind at all.

Hoisting 585 square feet of gaff-headed sail by yourself is good exercise. It is one reason why Arthur Cotta, in his mid-70s and with a heart condition, was feeling that *Sea Cat* was too much for him, and he was considering a fiberglass 18-footer. "Take it easy," he said, as I began hauling away on throat and peak halyards. It was rather like doing many curls with a pair of 25- or 30-pound dumbbells. The sail seemed to go on and on in endless yards of eight-ounce Dacron with a yellow-eyed cat's-head insignia staring blankly out of its midst.

With the centerboard down, *Sea Cat* draws about six feet of water. Cotta shut down the Palmer and we beat into the light breeze, all that remained of the strong winds. Despite her size, *Sea Cat* feels surprisingly light underway. We moved easily along, and as the wind began to gust up again, *Sea Cat*'s high bow and deep cockpit imparted a great sense of security. I clambered out to the pulpit and stood suspended there over the dark water, trying to picture a big swordfish lazing along beneath us.

It began to gust harder, to a solid 25, we guessed later, and the dark clouds of an approaching cold front rolled in low above the harbor. *Sea Cat* began getting cranky and taking control. Cotta was forced to ease her up in the puffs, and when the breeze developed a sustained force, he said it was time to lower sail and power home. We dropped all that square footage of Dacron into the lazyjacks and gathered it up as best we could, steering back toward Winthrop. It took us almost an hour to put *Sea Cat* away that afternoon. Later, Cotta told me how he first got involved with catboats.

"I learned about them," he said, "from a genuine Cape Codder back in 1935. His name was Walter Sherman, and he used to sail with the Crosbys. One day I said, 'Walter, I want to get a boat. What kind do you think I should get?'"

Sherman said he didn't know much about Boston Harbor, but that in the waters around the Cape and the Vineyard, a catboat did just fine. He supposed it would do fine farther north, too.

"I got embarrassed," Cotta remembers. "I must have blushed when I heard this term *cat*boat, because I had no idea what it was. Walter's wife saw me blush. 'It's not what you think it is, Arthur,' she said. 'Tell him what it is Walter.' So he started to laugh, too, because he never meant to imply cat*house*, and he exclaimed, 'You never *heard* of a catboat!' I told him I hadn't, that I knew nothing about sailing, and he said, 'Well, I'll tell you right now. Go out and get yourself a catboat.' I said, 'Well, all right. I will. What do they look like, anyway?'"

He began his search in Beverly and worked his way through yacht clubs and mooring areas from there to Provincetown and back again. He found many sloops for sale, but no catboats. Finally, he gave up looking for a catboat and made plans to buy a 34-foot sloop in Duxbury. He drove to Duxbury three weekends in a row, but somehow, the sloop's owner never wanted to go out for a demonstration sail. On the third afternoon, Cotta suddenly saw a catboat sail past. He bought her. He returned to Duxbury with some friends who "were supposed to know about boats." Nobody brought a chart, and the crew promptly ran aground near Clark's Island as the tide ran out of Duxbury Bay.

When the tide came in and floated them, they raised sail, an experience Cotta

Sea Cat, *Arthur Cotta at the wheel. (Stan Grayson photo)*

still remembers vividly. It was a 420-square-foot sail. "What a confusion and mess when that sail went up," said Cotta. "In fact, in the excitement, one of them broke off the ignition key so we couldn't shut down the engine. When I saw that tremendous sail, I said, 'Jeez, I must have got the wrong boat.'" With that, he began his education in the sailing of catboats. He became a founding member of The Catboat Association in 1963.

Comparing his earlier Crosby with *Sea Cat*, Cotta said this: "The old one dragged her stern a bit. This boat goes like a fish that's greased."

He put a canvas cover over the steering wheel and we prepared to row ashore. "You know," Cotta said, "after all these years with this boat, I feel as though I know Charles Anderson. Obviously, I never met the man, but everything I've done, I've tried to do in a way I think he would have approved."

He rowed us ashore, and as he rowed, I looked back at *Sea Cat*. She is an imposing vessel, and with a strong crew or a capable young owner, she would make a comfortable, able cruising boat, just what her owner had in mind when he bought her so many years before. But it is one of Arthur Cotta's great regrets that, after all his years of work, devotion, and dreaming, things failed to work out as he had hoped. He had time only for daysailing in *Sea Cat*. He never made a single cruise or spent a night aboard. The last time we talked, he said the boat had been sold.

8

Peggotty

$\mathbf{F}$ROM THE BOATBUILDER'S HOUSE in Westport, Massachusetts, to Little Compton, Rhode Island, was a drive of some 20 minutes. In the thin sunshine of an early spring afternoon, cows grazed on neatly fenced fields. The trees were still bare in mid-April, and in the distance, toward Newport, bays and rivers gleamed a cold gray. The Wilbor House, home of the Little Compton Historical Society, is a building behind a neat wall of smooth brown stones. During the off-season, the house is unannounced by any markers, and when I missed it for a third time, I stopped to ask a man plucking brush from his muddy garden.

"Let's see," he said. "I always have to think just how many houses away it is." He gathered up some wiry branches, paused, and said, "Six." Then he paused again. "Or seven. It's the sixth or seventh house up the road there."

"What color is it?"

"Well," he said, "it's colorless."

I thanked him and drove slowly back up Route 77 again, counting houses. I recognized the place, in the end, by its ancient-looking well. In fact, I had not come to see the house, built in 1689 by Samuel Wilbor and added to thereafter by subsequent generations. I had come instead to see what was out back. It rested there beneath the overhang of an old barn, where plows or a wagon would once have been kept. I had seen old catboats turned into flower planters or storage places for lobster pots, and I had seen them decaying in peace amid the bright grass of salt marshes, but I had never seen a catboat like the one in the vehicle shed

107

Peggotty *"on the hard" in Sydney Burleigh's backyard during the years he used her as his studio. (Courtesy Paul Darling and the Little Compton Historical Society)*

behind Samuel Wilbor's old house. A little sign told the story: "Catboat of 1850. Artist's Studio, 1906."

The artist who turned the catboat into a studio was named Sydney Burleigh. He was born in 1856, the son of a Little Compton farmer, and he became a painter whose watercolors and oils now hang in the State Museum in Providence and in some private collections. Burleigh spent much of his working life in Providence with his wife, also a painter. Together they established a studio that still stands, the Fleur de Lys Studio.

Each summer, Burleigh returned to Little Compton to paint landscapes of a countryside that remains bucolic to this day. On his journeys home, he crossed Sakonnet Passage aboard a small ferry that made the trip several times each week. Mostly, the boat carried produce from the rich farms above the river, but it occasionally carried passengers, too.

Beginning sometime in the 1850s, the boat used for this ferrying was a catboat of a type then in fairly wide use around the Newport area. Mostly, boats of this sort were called "Newport fish and lobster boats." It is unknown just how long this catboat served as the ferry at Sakonnet Passage. Burleigh referred to the boat as being "old" in the 1870s. At some point, the little craft was finally retired. Unceremoniously grounded out on the riverbank, she decayed slowly, leaving her ribs and planks like old bones in the mud and grass beside the water.

One day in 1906, Burleigh took a long look at the abandoned boat and, in a rush of fond inspiration, decided to take her home. He put the hull in his backyard and proceeded to turn it into what it remained forever after, a comfortable studio whose dimensions could be measured not just in terms of length and width, but as length overall, waterline length, beam, and draft. On the gunwales was erected a house of wide planks into which were cut various square, opening ports hung on black iron hinges, a bay window, and, at the stern, windows that ran across the entire transom, much like the windows in the sterncastle of some ancient galleon. A Dutch door was built in amidships on the starboard side, and a rose trellis was built alongside it. Then a thatched roof was added, giving the whole assembly the flavor of a nautical haystack.

Burleigh named his creation after that kindly soul described by David Copperfield's Aunt Betsy as "that out-of-the-way woman with the savagest of names." Her house "was a black barge or some other kind of superannuated boat ... high and dry on the ground with an iron funnel sticking out of it for a chimney and smoking very cozily. . . . There was a delightful door cut in the side, and it was roofed in, and there were little windows in it, but the wonderful charm of it was that it was a real boat, which had no doubt been upon the water hundreds of times, and which had never been intended to be lived in on dry land."

Burleigh named his boat *Peggotty*. He painted the name on the transom, installed a woodstove with a stovepipe chimney that stuck out through the roof, and worked aboard happily until his death in 1936. His wife lived to be 101, and it was she who gave *Peggotty* to the Historical Association, which knows a good deal about Burleigh but comparatively little about his studio.

As a matter of fact, nobody knows very much about *Peggotty* or boats like her. They were used so hard, so long ago, that only one is known to have survived. *It* rests in the small-boat shed at Mystic Seaport. As for *Peggotty*, she is as landbound as she is quaint. When she was moved by the Historical Association, her keel stayed in the mud of Burleigh's backyard, leaving her quite spineless and in need of careful blocking up in her new home. There she sits in peace, her days upon the Sakonnet River long over, her early history quite forgotten.

The boat at Mystic was built by a diminutive fisherman named William Munroe. He was raised by a Newport fisherman named John Swan and this, together with William's small size, earned him the nickname everybody knew him by. People called him Button Swan. Swan grew up sailing boats like *Peggotty*, and eventually, he built them. Christopher Grant La Farge was an admirer of Swan's, and in 1921 he wrote an article for *Scribner's* magazine that described these boats in general terms.

He wrote of them as follows: "Sixteen feet, sometimes eighteen was the standard length; rather broad, and with a low free-board. Lap straked, and no part decked over; fairly deep keel and inside ballast under the floor. There were two thwarts, the longitudinal space between them occupied by a well, boxed in like a centerboard casing, and divided by a fore and aft partition into two compartments. The well, from holes in the bottom of the boat, remained always full to the load waterline of clear green sea water. Abaft this, what may be called the cockpit with transoms. The mast stepped clean in the bows just forward of a third short thwart, and held in place by a hinged iron clamp, so arranged that it was quickly cast off and the mast taken down and laid lengthwise of the boat to make her ride at anchor

Lacking her keel, Peggotty *is now displayed at the Little Compton Historical Society. (Stan Grayson photo)*

more easily in a seaway. The rig was of the simplest, a mainmast with single halyard and a mainsheet. The sheet was made fast not to a cleat, but to a pin under the rail . . . . There were sweeps and thole pins for rowing and a scull hole alongside the rudder."

Boats of this type predate the centerboard, carvel-planked Newport catboats by some 12 to 20 years, assuming one accepts that the Newport fish and lobster boats appeared in the late-1840s and that the centerboard catboats began to appear in the mid-1860s, when Nathanael Herreshoff built *Sprite*.

The boat at Mystic exhibits most of the qualities La Farge describes, although she is smaller than was typical, being just over 12 feet long and with a comparatively narrow uncatboatlike beam of five feet four inches. In fact, when historian Howard Chapelle included the boat's lines in *American Small Sailing Craft*, he called *Button Swan* a Providence River boat, leading one to conclude that there were minor differences between this species and a Newport fish and lobster boat. According to Chapelle, Swan built the 12-footer in Saunderstown in 1875. Mystic Seaport acquired her 74 years later when she was removed from storage in a Saunderstown barn. Eventually the boat was restored with funds donated by The Catboat Association.

By the time restoration was complete, the man who did the work decided he wanted to learn more about boats like *Button Swan*. He drove to Little Compton and began piecing together *Peggotty*'s lines. The boatbuilder's name was Bob Baker. He had learned his trade from the old-time boatbuilders in Westport, Massachusetts, where he grew up. Baker seemed like an old-time boatbuilder himself, with his beard and pipe and quiet ways. That he valued simplicity was evident from the sort of boats he built and restored—small, graceful craft built of wood. The button he wore on his baggy sweater made a stronger statement than one was likely to hear Baker utter personally—"Question Authority."

When measuring *Peggotty*, Baker found he had many questions himself. Researching an old boat that is missing its keel and part of its stem requires some disciplined imagination. That is what Baker used when it came to drawing *Peggotty*'s shape below the waterline—that and reference to *Button Swan* and old photographs.

"The measuring didn't take long," he remembered of the project. "Drawing it did."

During his study of *Peggotty*, Baker was able to piece together a plausible history of the boat. Portions of a fish well remained, indicating to Baker that she "must have fished for a hell of a while." He found evidence that a half-deck had been installed, only to be cut out later so that a cabin could be added, presumably to provide some shelter on the boat's trips back and forth across the Sakonnet. Overall, Baker concluded that "the details of construction and general layout are the same as those of the *Button Swan* boat of 1870, indicating this style of boat was in use around Newport for some time."

By the time he had finished measuring, fairing lines, referring to *Button Swan*'s drawings, and thoughtfully filling in the blanks presented by *Peggotty*, Baker had created the lines for just the sort of boat described by La Farge. The drawings revealed a boat of prodigious beam for her length, yet a hull that possessed rather

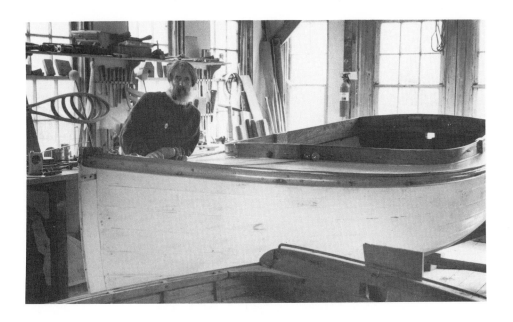

Bob Baker, builder of the new Peggotty, *in his shop with a Crosby catboat undergoing restoration, spring 1983. (Stan Grayson photo)*

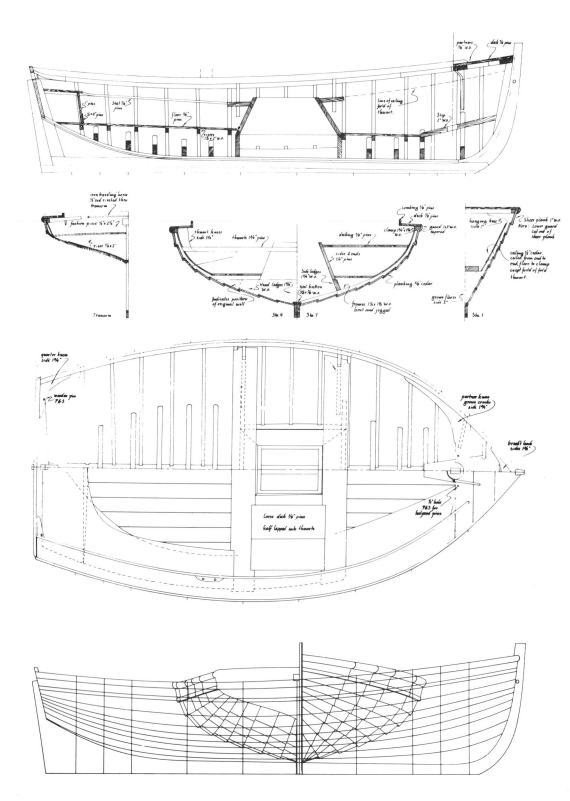

Construction drawings, layout, and lines of Peggotty *as drawn by Bob Baker. (Courtesy Mrs. Robert H. Baker)*

fine lines below the waterline. She had no centerboard. The sail plan, based on old engravings of boats in Newport Harbor, showed a gaff rig with a single halyard. What Bob Baker had done was to create drawings of a typical Newport fish and lobster boat that were as authentic as anyone is ever likely to achieve. When the drawings were complete, he rolled them up and put them away. He had no plans to build such a boat. He was content to have satisfied his curiosity and to have added to his own knowledge and that of other small-craft enthusiasts and marine historians. Then, one December day in 1977, a man named Charles Lee drove up to Baker's house. *That* was how *Peggotty* came to be reborn.

Charles Lee worked in the admissions department at St. George's School in Newport and liked old-fashioned boats. He once had owned a Kingston lobsterboat and, sometime later, decided he'd like to have a catboat. He had grown up sailing Beetle Cats and now wanted something that had plenty of room for his family without having great overall size. In fact, he had the plans for a catboat with him when he walked into Baker's boatshop. The builder, however, did not like the boat, which had been designed by R.D. ("Pete") Culler.

"He thought the boat was too frilly, too cute," said Lee.

Baker was just questioning an old authority, perhaps. Lee asked him what sort of catboat he *did* prefer.

"Well," said Baker, "I just finished taking the lines off a boat called *Peggotty*. . . ."

The two men sat down and contemplated the plans Baker had only recently completed. The lines, carefully inked, impressed Lee with their beauty. He went home to think about it for a time, returning once or twice to discuss various aspects of the project. He had never thought of owning a catboat like this, but, the more he thought about it, the better he liked it. He liked the idea of owning a boat indigenous to the area around Conanicut and Jamestown where he would be sailing. He liked the boat's looks and he liked Bob Baker. One day he told Baker, "Let's just go ahead and do this project."

"That's how it happened," he remembered, "just as simple as that."

The boat was built of southern cedar planks over oak frames. A substantial oak keel formed *Peggotty*'s backbone, and oak was used for the knees that supported the deck. "We'd go in the woods with a truck, a friend of Bob's, and a pattern," said Lee. "We'd take the pattern right up to an oak and cut the tree down. Then there was a big storm and a lot of big oak trees blew down and we got more oak that way."

As the project continued, *Peggotty* began to impress Baker and his assistant, Kevin Dwyer, as a very large 17-foot sailboat. More and more wood disappeared into her, and she grew to nearly overwhelm what had always seemed a reasonably spacious shop. Steaming and notching the frames to fit the lapped planks was a frustrating job that took three full days of labor and laments. The hull's curves, so beautiful to contemplate, made bending the cedar planks an exercise in deftness and precision. Sometimes, the wood proved too brittle for the task.

"We lost one of the garboards when we first tried to install it," remembered Baker. "It just kind of shattered." He was able to install planks at the rate of two per day, and gradually, as the weeks passed, *Peggotty* took shape. Baker tried to build her using materials as much like the original as possible. Where driftbolts were called for, he used wrought-iron bolts made in a local forge, driving the bolts into holes coated liberally with red lead to protect the metal from rust. The nails used for the planks were made of copper, although Baker thinks the original boats were fastened with bronze.

Red lead was used as a primer for the bottom prior to brushing on the copper paint, which Baker believes will attack untreated wood. According to La Farge, boats like this "were always painted dark green, the upper strake white, and a line or so of bright red or yellow inboard, according to the owner's fancy."

Sydney Burleigh's fancy had been to paint the boat's inside dark green, but Baker found a shade of buff or yellow beneath it. That is what he painted *Peggotty*'s interior, decks, and coamings. He used dark gray for the sole and a somewhat lighter gray for the topsides. A pleasant red was used on the gunwales.

"The paint job," said Charles Lee, "was as close as we could figure it."

The building of *Peggotty* was, in the end, a seven-month process during which Lee came to admire Baker as "an artist and craftsman who loves boats and is great to work with—if you have patience. *Peggotty* is a big boat. It doesn't look like a big boat. But there is a *ton* of boat there."

Lee was patiently awaiting completion of his unusual new boat when he decided to accept a job offer that would take him and his family to Hong Kong for three years. All through the spring of 1978, Baker and Kevin Dwyer worked long hours, seven days a week, until a time in August when *Peggotty*, with a cedar mast installed but lacking rigging and a rudder, was launched. The Lees departed for Hong Kong without ever getting to sail the boat.

That was left to Bob Baker. He built a rudder shaped like the one for *Button Swan*, since Burleigh's boat had no rudder to use as a guide, and he rigged the boat and bent on her vertically cut cotton sail made in Fairhaven by Smith Yacht Sails. The running rigging is the simplest imaginable. A single halyard suffices to raise the sail. The boom is rigged with the mainsheet. There is no topping lift. Baker's comment on the rig: "It seems very practical."

Baker took *Peggotty* down to Mystic Seaport, where she was moored near the whaleship *Charles W. Morgan* and sailed by Seaport staff members. She remained on display there until 1981, when Charles Lee returned to the United States and took his boat back to Rhode Island. Four years after he gave Bob Baker the go-ahead to build the boat, he at last had his first chance to discover something about how she sailed.

Here is what C. Grant La Farge had to say about the sailing qualities of boats like *Peggotty*: "They made well to windward if not pinched too close; they were quite fast for their size and rather short rig, off the wind; quick and reliable in stays, and very stiff. They did not smash and pound into the seas, but rode quietly and smoothly over them."

This is what Charlie Lee had to say about *Peggotty* before we went sailing together: "This boat is not easy to sail. It's not a Beetle or a 470. You have to think ahead, and if you make a mistake, it goes *through* docks."

The boat that demolished docks if you weren't careful lay innocently on her mooring. My first impression, as we rowed out in Charlie Lee's Zodiac inflatable, was of how gracefully her planks were curved. The vessel possessed, too, a certain undeniable air of antiquity. It was as if we were rowing toward another century. This sense of going back in time became even stronger when we stepped aboard,

"Ready about!" Builder Bob Baker tacks Peggotty *during sea trials on the Barrington River in 1977. Here the boat's great beam carried well aft, her simple finish, and the single-halyard rig are readily apparent. (Paul Darling photo)*

for I had never imagined a boat quite so simply fitted as this one. The unfinished cedar mast had great checks in it that Charlie Lee has ceased worrying about. In the boat's middle was an enormously wide central thwart with its built-in fish well. The well was not open to the sea but was used instead for storage. Like the Newport boats of old, *Peggotty* possessed not a single cleat. The halyard belayed onto an unfinished pin, and there was no standing rigging at all, not even a headstay.

"You have to keep telling yourself," said Charlie Lee, "that this boat is a throwback in time. Remember, when Bob Baker took the lines off the original *Peggotty*, her hull was at least 125 years old." He lifted a couple of the gray-painted floorboards to show me the ballast. It was rock ballast that came from a copper smelter's slag heap. The copper leaches out and helps prevent rot.

Not much was necessary to get *Peggotty* ready to sail. Charlie tied off the dinghy to the mooring painter and uncoiled the sheet, while I hauled away on the halyard, raised the sail, and belayed the halyard to the pin. We cast off, and in the absence of any wind, started drifting toward a long wooden pier. Charlie said I could try out the 14-foot sweep if I wanted. I unlashed it, put it in the thole pins, and rowed for a while, long enough to convince myself that *Peggotty* is indeed a lot of boat.

"The old-timers may have sculled, which would have made more sense," said Lee.

After a while, we accepted a tow out to a breath of wind. Then, slowly, we edged over toward Newport, barely moving across Narragansett Bay. When it really blows, Lee said he finds the boat entirely able and safe, although she quickly gets overwhelming if not reefed. Fishermen like Button Swan took their boats out daily to challenge the reefs, rocks, and currents of the bay and Brenton Reef.

"Fishing, for that breed of men, was something that meant niceties of accurate boat handling beyond the comprehension of those who haul pots and traps with engine-propelled craft," wrote La Farge.

Swan could find his way as unerringly as if equipped with some internal Loran-C. "He knew the bottom of those waters," wrote La Farge, "as you know the stairs in your house."

From boats like *Peggotty*, Swan and men like him could earn a living, handlining for bluefish, flounder, bass, and cod, baiting their hooks with lobster and menhaden as they sailed about the edges of dangerous ledges, turning the tide and wind to their advantage as if by instinct, all in boats that, even in the 1870s, must have been deemed primitive.

By the time we had sailed and drifted our way over to Fort Adams, the wind began to increase very slightly. *Peggotty*, with her long keel, tracked well, and inside Newport Harbor, showed she would go to windward reasonably if you didn't try to force the issue and pinch her up too much. She could make progress to windward against the tide despite the light breeze, but if trimmed too much, she would slow and then lose ground, falling off to leeward until the sheet was eased and she gathered way again. Charlie Lee said the boat suffered most when going to windward in a chop.

"The bows are bluff," he said, "and she just stops."

This apparent fault seems to have had little significant impact on those who actually *used* boats like this. With patience and craft, they turned the boats' strong

Charlie Lee at the tiller of Peggotty. *(Stan Grayson photo)*

points, their seaworthiness and ability off the wind, to good advantage. They knew how to balance nature's forces against the boats' abilities. Lee himself has made a passage from Stonington to Newport, having a fine time and convincing himself that the boat is not a passagemaker, but that she could do such a trip safely. The only real improvement he thinks about is a larger rudder.

"There are times when it's blowing hard," he said, "that she feels a bit out of control."

On the way back to Jamestown, the wind picked up some more, blowing out of the south, giving us a beam reach and letting *Peggotty* show off. We sailed along, delighted. A 12-meter passed, heading toward Newport after a day's practice. In comparison with other boats, the Twelve seemed jet-propelled. As she went by us, our little catboat seemed more than ever what she was, a practical, unpretentious dinosaur.

In 1921, 16 years after Button Swan died, C. Grant La Farge remembered Swan's era, and his own youth, as a time when everything "seemed a part of the natural, settled, permanent order of life." But that order did not remain much past the turn of the century. It was changed forever, not so much by the development of more sophisticated boats as by the advent of the gasoline engine. After that, nothing was ever the same again. "He is gone," wrote La Farge of Button Swan. "The seaworthy little craft have vanished as completely as the long ships of the Vikings."

For 60 years after La Farge lamented the passing of the boats, men, and fishing he had loved, that was true. Now there is *Peggotty* to remind us.

Cap Phinney and Matchless

I N THE SPRING OF 1891, Grover Cleveland, who had served as 22nd president of
the United States, bought a picturesque wooden cottage just north of
Monument Beach on Cape Cod. Cleveland called his house Gray Gables, and each
summer he and his family journeyed there to enjoy the privacy Cleveland always
sought and the fishing he took as seriously as tariffs. "If you want to catch fish," he
told his friend, newspaper editor Richard Watson Gilbert, "attend strictly to
business."

Grover Cleveland did much of his fishing from a catboat. Named *Ruth* for
Cleveland's first child, this was a boat whose ancestry has gone unrecorded, but it
bore a resemblance to Crosby designs. The President was photographed once
aboard *Ruth*, his ample belly thrusting above the companionway. Cleveland
bought Gray Gables after he narrowly lost his bid for reelection in 1888, and he
quickly developed an attachment for the Cape and its people, as well as its fish. He
expressed surprise that this beautiful place had not been overrun much as, after
1889, Oklahoma was overrun by homesteaders.

"We keep the waters of Buzzards Bay clean and pure for fishing purposes, and
do not propose to have our resource stirred up and contaminated by the inflow of
other waters through the Cape Cod Canal." He opposed the canal.

Cleveland was friendly with his neighbors, whether they were wealthy like John
Forbes on Naushon Island, boatmen like Captain Ryder with whom he often sailed,
or local boatbuilders like C.C. Hanley and his family. Even before they bought Gray
Gables, Cleveland and his wife were enough a part of the community to be asked to

119

attend local events, and that is how Francis Cleveland came to present trophies for a catboat race held by the Sippican Yacht Club in Marion in 1887. Winner of second place was a near neighbor of the Clevelands in Monument Beach, a boatbuilder who shared the President's love for children and his uncompromising moral standards. This man was William Wallace Phinney.

W.W. Phinney, whom most people referred to as "Cap Phinney," was born in South Monument in June 1865, not long after Lee surrendered to Grant at Appomattox. Phinney's father had served in the Union navy and Phinney was named for an uncle who enlisted in the Union army, was captured at Jacksonville in 1864, escaped and was recaptured, only to perish before the war's end. The Phinneys had long been settled in that part of Cape Cod south of Sandwich, and the harbor at Monument Beach still bears the family name. It is Phinneys Harbor.

When Cap Phinney paused, late in life, to reflect upon the past, he recorded that his first six years had been uneventful but that when he was seven, he was kicked by a horse, and at eight, he was bitten by a dog. He built his first boat when he was 13, and at 16 he was sailing parties aboard a 24-foot catboat. He did not graduate from Wareham High School but instead became an apprentice of Frederick Dunn, a Monument Beach boatbuilder who introduced Phinney to boat design and construction. By the time Phinney was 17, he was fishing from his own catboat during summer and fall, working in a shoe factory, and doing whatever else was necessary to earn an honest living. Once he picked 135 quarts of blueberries in a single day.

At age 21, Phinney married. He built a 30- by 17-foot boatshop in Monument Beach, and together with a partner named William Buzzell began a career he would pursue for the next half century. It was with one of his first boats, *Superior*—built apparently with the help of both Dunn and Buzzell—that he won the Sippican Yacht Club trophy. Phinney never lost his taste for racing, and over the years he acquired an impressive trophy collection. When he won the Atlantic Coast Catboat Championship in 1911, the commodore of the Boston Yacht Club presented him with a brass clock. This clock and Phinney's other awards, along with the half-models he carved for his robust boats, are now scattered, but they remain in the hands of his descendants. He sailed in races on Cape Cod, Buzzards Bay, and around Boston, making with some regularity the two-day trip around the Cape to Boston Harbor. On one of those trips, he encountered what he always called his worst storm at sea. Aboard a 24-foot catboat, he said he weathered an 80-knot gale.

In his shop at Monument Beach, Phinney practiced the strict manners and morals he'd been brought up with and those he heard preached at the Methodist church. He was a regular churchgoer and did such woodworking as the church required. Eventually he built an altar for the First Methodist Church in Bourne. Said a local newspaper of the boatbuilder, "Cleanliness of thought and moral deed are his goals. . . . Finding himself slipping into slovenly speech habits, he once told a group of his men in the midst of an important job that they must stop using dirty speech and telling tainted stories or he would have to stop work. Men often speak of him now as a man who never lets his tongue slip. . . ."

To the boys of the neighborhood, Phinney was known simply as "Gramps." He took time to answer their many questions and to help them with their yacht models, scallop boxes, and quahog rakes. He also instructed them in his rigorous

Cap Phinney. (Courtesy Mrs. Gladys Perry)

standards of "manliness and morals." When W.W. grew old and was afflicted by arthritis, the kids who frequented his shop fetched his tools to save the old man extra labor. "We *lived* in that yard," said one, years later.

Phinney labored hard and earned a reputation as an efficient, quick craftsman even though he always shunned most power tools. Merton Long, who worked with Phinney to learn boatbuilding, said Phinney once told him he "had sawed his way to New York and home again."

"A regular day for him was 12 hours," Long once told Catboat Association founder John Leavens. "Phinney was a fine man to work for, never cross or cranky, all the time happy and joking. He loved to have men come in to talk of catboats and of racing them. He was an expert sailor himself and would rather race than eat." Sometimes, he went over to Osterville and talked boatbuilding with his friend Wilton Crosby.

He was generous, too. Ted Palmer, one of those who sat in Phinney's shop for hours as a youngster, remembered that the boatbuilder would lend a boat to the Sea Scouts in the summer and that he made available two 16-foot catboats so that Palmer and his brother could give sailing lessons to Girl Scouts from a nearby camp. Like everyone who ever knew Phinney, Palmer remembers him as devout, a sort of archetypal Cape Cod Christian, and a fine sailor.

Captain W.W. Phinney poses with Oriole, *his last catboat, on launch day, 1940, Falmouth. (Courtesy John William Brackett)*

"Cap Phinney always said he could build a catboat to win the [America's] Cup races," said Palmer, "and because he was quite a sailor, we didn't doubt it."

In 1913 Phinney sold his shop to a former state governor who demanded an unimpeded water view from his own house. Then Phinney moved to Falmouth, where he established himself anew. He attracted additional enthusiastic youngsters, continued his abstemious ways, and took every opportunity to eat peach ice cream, play checkers, or go out formally attired for drives in his Buick coupe, slipping the clutch mercilessly. He never was entirely comfortable with machines.

The number of boats Phinney built during his career is unknown. He retired in the mid-1930s after working a lifetime of 12-hour days, but if any records of this work were kept, they have disappeared. Phinney himself guessed he had built about 100 boats, including life-saving pulling boats used in the Charles River Basin, catboats of all sizes, and a 53-foot schooner. He retired because of his arthritis and sold the yard (it is now known as MacDougalls'), but almost immediately he became restless. He drove around Falmouth then, spending hours talking with old friends, and soon began carving a half-model that served as the basis for one last catboat. It was launched on his 75th birthday, christened with a ginger ale bottle filled with harbor water.

"He built his last boat," said his daughter Gladys, "as busywork, a hobby."

This last boat, a 29-foot keel catboat that Phinney called *Oriole*, was constructed in a one-time dancehall with doors so small that everyone wondered

*In the light air of a late summer
afternoon, the Phinney catboat*
Mayflower *breasts a flood tide on
the Parker River near Newbury,
Massachusetts. Built circa 1909,
this keel catboat was used once
for fishing. Her original rig was
apparently greatly reduced in
size, making the hefty 30-footer
slow in light air, but she otherwise
closely resembles the* Oriole, *built
some 30 years later. Here she sets
a small jib in an effort to increase
performance. (Stan Grayson
photo)*

how the boat would ever be removed. When the time came, Phinney removed one
wall. He was as meticulous about *Oriole*'s construction as he'd been about all his
other boats, and he sailed her frequently, limping about her big cockpit, until he
finally decided to cease going sailing. When he demonstrated the boat to its new
owner, "it was blowing half a gale, but he had no notion of putting in a reef. . . . She
stood it all right but it was hair raising."

After *Oriole*, Phinney built no more boats, and he was distressed by those he
saw launched by others during the last years of his life. "It's disgusting," he told a
reporter in 1940, "the way boats are slapped together today. A banana crate, a
dash of glue, and a flashy veneer, and you have a new streamliner. The old way of
making boats with the accent on individual craftsmanship assured a long vigorous
life. Look at me. You wouldn't say I was slapped together in a hurry. Same with the
craft we used to build."

Because Phinney's boats were never "slapped together," several of them lasted
for quite a long time. A number of devoted owners have cared for *Oriole*, and she is
in commission today in the hands of a skipper impressed by her rock-hard oak
frames, stout pine planking, and galvanized iron fastenings. At the time he built
Oriole, Phinney discovered a barrel of rosin floating offshore, and he melted down
the rosin and poured it waxlike into the boat's bottom so that water would not
collect anywhere on the wooden planking. But *Oriole*, now *Snow Goose*, is, at age

43, comparatively young. Sometime around 1908, Phinney launched a 27-foot centerboard catboat that he promptly raced against a boat built by Horace Crosby. As far as anybody now knows, the new boat's name was indicative of its success, and the name has remained unchanged ever since. Phinney named this boat *Matchless.*

When Bill Moore was a child, his family summered on Cape Cod. These vacations had two long-lasting results. Moore became fascinated with gasoline engines and with catboats. He bought his first engine, a jump-spark-ignition, one-cylinder, two-cycle of unknown manufacture, in Winthrop. It cost three dollars, which, Moore recalls, was "a lot of money in those days."

The engine was in pieces. Moore took it home in a basket, and his father, who owned a small machine shop, helped him rebuild it. They installed the engine in a 12-foot flat-bottomed skiff, and Moore began making little excursions from Waquoit Bay to the Vineyard and other nearby ports. There was an old fisherman who would sometimes invite Moore to accompany him in his catboat. It too was fitted with a one-lunger, a fine make-and-break Lathrop. Moore stared in delight as the old boatman pushed down on the oiler to squirt lubricant into the cylinder while the make-and-break igniter hammered away in a blur of steel.

"I thought that was one better than our jump spark," said Moore. "That make-and-break was *it*, the top of the ladder." At an early age, he became a sort of mechanical elitist, and he never lost his love for old gas engines. Today, he goes to old-engine meets where enthusiasts, often wearing engineer hats, walk about looking at brightly painted machines from another age. Moore takes lawn chairs and a sun awning to the meets, and his wife, Millie, takes her knitting. Together they have what they both agree is "a really nice time."

At about the same time he began to appreciate engines, Moore found himself growing increasingly aware of catboats. He appreciated what the boats had to offer, being capable of standing up to rough weather while also able to exploit shoal water. "I thought they were beautiful," he said, "and that someday I'd have a catboat of my own."

Thirty-six years later, he decided to sell the sloop he then owned and buy the catboat he had wanted ever since he was a boy. He and his wife searched for just the right catboat for months, beginning in 1975. They flew their light plane, a Cessna 170, up and down the East Coast, investigating possibilities. They placed an ad in *The Catboat Association Bulletin*, saying they wanted a wooden catboat, and one day, they got a reply from a man who said he had been restoring an old wooden boat and that it was now for sale.

"My wife said," remembered Moore, "that we weren't going to look at any old boat, but I argued that we should at least go to *look* at it."

They have never forgotten the day they first saw the boat. "We walked up over this hillcrest," said Millie Moore, "and honestly, we just went 'aaahh.'"

"What we did," said her husband, "we just fell in love with that boat."

They told the owner what they were prepared to spend, but he said he wanted more. The Moores spent a sleepless night and went back to look at *Matchless* a second time. They reviewed again all the work Roger Judge, the owner, had done. After he had bought the boat from a man who could not afford needed repairs, he

Bill and Millie Moore aboard Matchless. *(Stan Grayson photo)*

proceeded to install 30 partial frames and many planks over a three-year period. He installed a new caprail on the coaming and discovered cutouts there for oarsockets, suggesting that, even on large catboats, such fittings were considered necessary. Much of the wood was original, but there was much that was new. The centerboard had been cut down in size and the entire cabin had been modified at some point to increase headroom while eliminating the previously graceful merging of cockpit coaming and cabin side.

"I didn't have the ambition to take all that apart and redo it," said Roger Judge. "I never would have finished."

After looking at the boat again, the Moores agreed to buy her. "We decided," they said, "that you only go this way once, so we went home that night and said 'OK.'" They called Judge to let him know they would meet his price, but he said that he was sorry, that somebody else had come by and actually put a deposit on the boat.

"There are other boats," he told them sympathetically. "You'll find one you like."

Millie Moore remembers that she cried herself to sleep that night. Then, she and her husband climbed back into their little airplane and began hopping around again, to Martha's Vineyard, Connecticut, and other places where catboats were listed for sale. "We looked," said Millie, "but we never found one we liked."

For the Moores, it seemed, the old boat Cap Phinney had built was, indeed, matchless. "There was just something about it," said Bill Moore, "that we loved. Every bit of it, the shape of the stern, the bow, just everything, including the size. It's like a beautiful woman: There's no way you can improve her." Still, the couple had given up on buying *Matchless* by the time the owner called one day to say his buyer could not raise the necessary money. The asking price had crept upward, too, but the Moores did not hesitate. In the summer of 1976, they became, as nearly as they could determine, the boat's ninth owners.

At the time the Moores bought *Matchless*, the boat was 70 years old. She had survived all the great storms of the century. Once, in 1954, Hurricane Carol swept her up a lane in Barrington, Rhode Island, and dumped her, mast broken, between two telephone poles beside a house. The survey Moore commissioned revealed much about the boat and Phinney's construction methods. The frames were 1⅞-inch by 2-inch hard pine on 10-inch centers; the planks were 1⅛-inch cedar fastened with wrought-iron nails. Before *Matchless* was offered for sale to the Moores, many of the frames had been strengthened with doublers. The deck beams and stem were made of oak. The current Douglas fir mast, brightly varnished, had been fashioned from the spinnaker boom of the J boat *Resolute*, which had successfully defended the America's Cup against *Shamrock IV* in 1920. A new centerboard had been built, and the Gray engine was found to be in excellent condition.

The surveyor's report concluded: "This is an old classic. It is an original old Phinney catboat, which has been completely rebuilt and refinished, and an exceptionally expert job done. It is almost impossible to put a price on a classic of this type in this kind of condition, and she is worth about what anyone is willing to pay."

This report did nothing to lessen the Moores' enthusiasm. They learned that a number of frames would eventually need strengthening, but this minor defect was nothing compared to what *Matchless* had going for her. After their long search, the Moores had come to own exactly the boat they wanted.

Bill Moore is a machinist and a very handy man. Once he designed and built a rotisserie for a customer who wanted to roast an entire lamb. When the old drawbridge between Portsmouth and Kittery broke down, it was Moore who got the job of building the enormous bronze bearings needed to make it operational. And, when a vital drawbridge in Lynn, Massachusetts, broke down, delaying for hours the Boston rush-hour traffic, Moore made the new part necessary for its repair. The newspapers said that the part was being made in a special machine shop in Pennsylvania, but it wasn't. It was made in Moore's shop in South Boston.

Despite his many skills, Moore does little of the maintenance on *Matchless*. This he prefers to leave to an old boatbuilder who once worked at Crosby's and who, during the winter and spring of 1982-83, made the last repairs suggested by the boat's survey. Of this builder, Moore said: "He doesn't drink and is very pious. He must be something like Cap Phinney." The work included several new planks for the forward sections, the sistering of several frames, and a general refinishing. *Matchless* did not go into the water until late June, but when she did, she was immaculate.

In hull form, *Matchless* seems typical of Phinney's centerboard designs, which were largely similar although their size ranged from some 16 to 27 feet. No lines for *Matchless*, or any other Phinney catboat, seem ever to have been taken. Phinney worked directly from his half-models, laying out the boats in half-inch squares and

Matchless. *Off Peddocks Island, Boston Harbor. (Stan Grayson photo)*

scaling these up full size on the shop floor. If lines were to be drawn, they would show a graceful sheer with modest freeboard, a flat run aft, a firm bilge, and a fine entrance. All this added up to a potentially fast, race-winning boat. By contrast, Phinney's keel catboats were more robust, with high freeboard. *Oriole* had a four-foot draft, and in common with other Phinney keel catboats, she did not earn a reputation for speed.

On a hot and humid day in July 1983, the Moores welcomed me aboard *Matchless* for a demonstration sail in Quincy Bay. The boat's cockpit is vast and could easily accommodate a party of eight or 10 people. The cabin, with its raised top, does not offer standing headroom but is a comfortable place nonetheless. It is ventilated through bronze opening ports. An enclosed, electrically operated head is in the forepeak. The earlier owner who reduced the size of the boat's centerboard also reduced the rig. Thus, in common with most old catboats, *Matchless*'s sail is not as large as Phinney intended, but Moore has found its 550 square feet to be ideal for cruising. He need not reef the boat until the wind is above 20 knots, and he never has missed the speed a larger sail plan would provide. The Moores have, by now, cruised *Matchless* over much of New England, including a trip to Maine.

"We'll pull in somewhere," said Moore, "and somebody might ask, 'Hey, is that the *Matchless* that was here in 1935?'"

Quick as a tick, the big Gray started; we backed out of the slip with the board down to aid maneuverability, and headed out of the marina. Moore does not know what kind of engine was fitted to *Matchless* originally, and Phinney himself never had a great deal to say about engines. Usually, he bored the shaft holes but then left installation to a Falmouth garage owner named John Barry. On those occasions when Phinney had to choose an engine, he usually opted for a Red Wing.

We raised sail just outside the marina. It went up easily on its hoops, the gaff riding on a saddle arrangement that replaces gaff jaws and has been found to be entirely satisfactory by the Moores. Soon we were reaching in light air past the homes and industries lining the shore and toward more open water and the many islands of Boston Harbor. Despite the light conditions, *Matchless* did not feel sluggish. We moved easily, and when it was necessary to trim the sail as we changed course to windward, the boat pointed nicely, so well that I began to wonder, of course, what she had been like with her original sail and centerboard. The sail is equipped with two sets of reef points, but Moore said that if it breezed up, he usually just dropped the sail and motored. He reported that on an occasion when he did put two reefs in, *Matchless* continued to handle well, and that the boat will still come about in such conditions.

Matchless carries no ballast aside from her engine, but Moore says he has never felt the need to add any. Certainly, on the day we sailed together, the boat felt stiff enough. Phinney used lead or beach stone in his boats, but how much of either material *Matchless* ever carried is unknown.

It was shortly after the noon hour when we nosed *Matchless* in toward a lunchtime anchorage off Peddocks Island. Moore took advantage of the boat's two-foot 10-inch draft to motor in quite close to the beach, and then dropped a Danforth anchor. A sportfisherman friend of the Moores stopped by, showed off a bucket full of fine flounder, and added a lobster he had hooked to our luncheon larder. Down in the cabin, Millie Moore boiled the lobster and served up a platter loaded with cheeseburgers and salad, which we ate while staring off at the many sails upon the bright green water. The day reminded the Moores of another, an August afternoon years earlier.

Then, they found themselves trudging up a hill overlooking a winding estuary near Marshfield, Massachusetts. They walked up the hill through clouds of persistent gnats, and when they reached the crest, they had their first eyeful of the boat they had come to see. Below them, glistening white in the sunshine, was *Matchless*.

10

C.C. Hanley and the Mollie B.

THE ROAD LEADING TO the farm is a dirt road. It runs in a reasonably straight line through the woods, past a sign that says "Danger, Corgi Crossing," and ends beneath a large tree beside the farmhouse. From here, high on a ridge near Blue Hill, one can see hundreds of acres of woods. On warm days in early fall, cloud puffs may float benignly in the sky above the bay, while sweet-smelling honeysuckle tumbles brightly at the barnyard fence. The draft horses moving slowly in a cleared field give the place its name—Horsepower Farm.

"The minute we appeared over the hill, we knew this was it," is how Paul Birdsall remembers his first look at the farm in 1972. That was a time before he truly comprehended the value of chicken manure as fertilizer or had fathomed the dozens of skills and tricks involved in training a horse to do good work.

"At that time," said Paul's wife, Mollie, looking off at the trees, "we were babes in the woods."

Only a few years after they bought their farm, however, the Birdsalls knew enough to lament the passing of the big chicken farms in nearby Belfast and were receiving applications from would-be apprentices eager to share Paul's expertise with draft horses and Mollie's market-garden skills. The Birdsalls came to Maine for the first time in the summer of 1967. They made the trip by boat and encountered so much fog that they had only one clear week in five. It was not until a return trip in 1969 that they really experienced Maine for the first time.

"We saw entire harbors we hadn't seen before," said Mollie.

These harbors, most of them remote and uncrowded, tantalized them. Each year that they cruised from their home in Middletown, Connecticut, to Cape Cod, they found the anchorages more crowded. Once, after a long approach to an apparently deserted, quiet Nauset Beach, they found the sands lined with beach buggies. "They had taken over," said Paul.

Maine began looking better and better to him, and he found himself facing a career decision. He could either continue to teach at the high school in Westport or complete his doctorate in Latin-American history with a goal of teaching it in college. But college teaching jobs were already scarce in 1971, and with his own work and Mollie's many activities tending to draw them apart, they decided to go to Maine.

"We felt," they agreed, "that if we lived here, we'd have something we could share." Their cruise to Maine in 1972 was really a journey in search of a new home. The first place in Blue Hill that the realtor took them was the farm.

The boat in which the Birdsalls cruised to Maine was an old cat yawl, an unusual vessel even when she was built in 1927. She seems to have made a lasting impression on everyone who ever saw her. When the Birdsalls first sailed to Monhegan, Mollie walked up the steep lane leading from the town dock and went to the store, where the shopkeeper asked her which boat she had arrived on.

"The cat yawl," she said.

"Well, it's funny," he replied. "That boat looks just like one called the *Two Sisters* that was built in Quincy when I was a boy. It was built for a wealthy doctor and all of us kids used to climb all over and see the whole process of what was going on."

That was the Birdsalls' boat, 40 years earlier.

Shortly after noon on a Saturday in September 1982, I left Horsepower Farm with the Birdsalls and two apprentices. Gear for a day's sail was packed into the car, and we set off for Center Harbor, where the boat, which Paul had named *Mollie B.*, was anchored. We intended to bring her home to Blue Hill. Paul drove down through South Blue Hill, where folksinger and recording artist Noel Stookey lives, and along tree-lined two-lanes until we passed E.B. White's house in Brooklin. When we got to the boatyard run by White's son Joel, we stopped. We piled all our gear into Paul's worn-looking Dyer dinghy, and he rowed out with Mollie to fetch the boat. The old yawl looked much like she had in her photos and plans—graceful, with a tumblehome stem and a large and airy-looking cabin. This was the last boat ever designed by Charles C. Hanley, the man who created the fastest catboats of all. As far as anybody knows, *Mollie B.* is the last Hanley boat that survives in more or less original form, and the only cat *yawl* he ever designed.

"If I were building a boat for myself," Hanley told a *Yachting* magazine writer when he was an old man, "to be able, safe and comfortable to handle alone if I liked, I'd build me a cat yawl, not over 30 feet; the little jigger will keep her easy on her mooring, and you'll have enough room for day sailing and cruising, you can go anywhere in her if you use good judgment and you'll find her handy. After all, the Cape Cat is just another good old Yankee notion—one pretty near giving a man his money's worth in a boat."

As we left Center Harbor, Paul Birdsall was talking about catboats, *Mollie B.*, draft horses, and Maine, all of which, to him, fit neatly under the same heading— "good old Yankee notions."

The good old Yankee who designed the Birdsalls' boat was born in Warren, Maine, in 1851. Because he achieved remarkable success in a highly visible sport, and because he just naturally made for a good interview, rather more is known about C.C. Hanley than about other catboat builders. One way or another, Hanley got to be famous. Eventually, he was commissioned to design and build an America's Cup boat, a *centerboard* America's Cup boat. Those close to the sport of yacht racing considered Hanley to be the Crosbys' chief rival, and yachting historian William P. Stephens summed up this rivalry by writing that "the Crosby cats were true to their lineage, always sturdy and powerful. Coming into the game in its racing stage, Hanley as a rule built lighter boats. He was an artist in the building of this size yacht, laying all the plank himself." His boats were commonly so well made that their seams remained invisible a decade or two after they were launched.

Charles Hanley started his career as an apprentice piano maker in Boston. There he learned to use each of the tools in the wooden tool chest given him by his father. By the time he was 24, Hanley had done all the piano-case building he wanted. He left Boston for Monument Beach, where he set up shop as a blacksmith. A year later he married, and at some point that neither Hanley nor anybody else ever bothered to note, he began watching and sailing in catboat races. By the early 1880s, he was building catboats of his own, combining an inherent sense of proportion and form with the woodworking skills he had mastered in Boston. There seems to have been nothing Hanley could not do. He was equally adept at forming up the case for a baby grand or at finishing off a yacht's cabin. In short order, his boats became known for their high level of craftsmanship.

These were expensive boats, about twice the cost of anything comparable in size. Hanley, an outgoing man who literally bet on his boats' ability to meet measurement rules and win races, probably believed his products had no rival in overall design and construction detail. In 1899, when he was commissioned on short notice to build a Canada's Cup entry, he made a model in one day and said he would forfeit $800 if the finished boat did not fit the rules. The resulting yacht was the 42-foot centerboarder *Genesee*. She did not lose a race in the series for which she had been built. *Clara*, a 28-foot catboat built in 1895, raced in 13 events around Boston, taking five firsts although she was sometimes raced *singlehanded* by her owner.

Although the lines of various Hanley boats were published in contemporary yachting magazines, Hanley apparently did his design work using beautifully carved half-models. He soon established a basic shape and stuck to it throughout his career. Rather than having plumb stems, his catboats had a tumblehome, canoelike bow profile typified by the *Mollie B*. The waterlines were hollow forward and there was obvious flare in the forward sections. Bilges were firm, deadrise shallow, and the freeboard was, in comparison with a typical Crosby catboat, reduced. Some of Hanley's boats had a barndoor rudder, others, a more graceful raised transom and underhung rudder. Overall lengths of 25 to 28 feet were typical of the racing catboats, built to basic class rules, and most of the boats carried inside ballast, although some had a lead ballast "keel" bolted to the wooden keel.

It was the 26½-foot *Mucilage*, built in 1888, that seems to have established

Fresh from the July 4, 1889 victory at Newport that established C.C. Hanley as a force in American yacht racing, Mucilage *sails a fast reach in Narragansett Bay. Sold by her first owner, the boat was renamed* Iris. *In 1906 she was returned to Massachusetts and fitted with new sails, and the following year, when she was 20 years old, she sailed in 31 races and won championships in three racing associations. (Nathaniel L. Stebbins photo. Courtesy of The Society for the Preservation of New England Antiquities)*

Hanley's name with racing sailors beyond the Cape and Buzzards Bay. He once said he gave the boat its name because he hoped "to stick the prize of every race on her." Hanley had raced her himself for a year when one of those "wealthy sportsmen of New York and Newport" so common to 19th-century yachting persuaded him to bring *Mucilage* to Newport. There, the boat raced against the best yachts in Rhode Island and defeated them by 20 minutes.

"For some time," noted C.C., "it was difficult to convince the judges we had been in the same race at all because of our advantage."

E.D. Morgan, the wealthy sport who had suggested Hanley enter the race, bought *Mucilage* on the spot. Hanley's next boat was even more successful, for she happened to arrive in the right place at just the right time. On July 15, 1889, she defeated, among others, two larger boats designed by two of the country's most famous yacht designers. This occurred right in that rockbound bastion of American sailboat racing, Marblehead.

The boat that did all this turned out to be aptly named by her owner, a member of the Hull Yacht Club. He called the boat *Harbinger*. With a length of 28 feet 10 inches overall—the waterline was 27 feet 9 inches—and a 13½-foot beam, *Harbinger* was certainly typical of Hanley's designs. She was one of his barndoor-rudder catboats, carrying a long bowsprit on which a jib and spinnaker could be set when reaching or running.

The dimensions of *Harbinger*'s rig are awesome to contemplate. Her mast was 40 feet high and her boom equally long, making it some 11 feet *longer* than the boat itself. The bowsprit projected 16 feet. The gaff was 28 feet. A long spinnaker pole was carried to allow *Harbinger* to set one of the triangular sails then referred to as a spinnaker. In all, this 28-foot catboat could spread 1,551 square feet of sail.

Had *Harbinger* merely dominated local catboat races, Hanley's reputation might have gotten no further than that one class of yacht. But in July, her owner entered her in a race sponsored by the Eastern Yacht Club in Marblehead. The race was certain to attract attention, since those who followed the sport were fascinated by the rivalry of two other boats in *Harbinger*'s class. These were the 30-foot-waterline cutter *Saracen*, designed by Edward Burgess and built by Lawley, and *Kathleen*, a 30-footer designed by William Gardner. These were both keel boats—*Kathleen* drew seven feet—that spread some 2,000 square feet of sail. Two famous 40-footers were in the race, too. These were the William Fife–designed *Minerva*, and *Papoose*, from Burgess's office.

Precisely what happened that rainy, misty day in July was well documented in newspaper and magazine accounts. *Harbinger*, still fresh from a victory on both corrected *and* elapsed time over the Herreshoff sloop *Nimbus*—which was considered a rival of Herreshoff's famous sloop *Shadow*—started the race with five others in her class. There was a strong wind blowing down from the northeast, and the keel cutters housed their topmasts.

All the boats experienced an eventful run down past Graves Light to the turning mark at Hardings Ledge, east of Hull. *Kathleen* attempted but failed to set her spinnaker, making do with main and jib topsail. *Harbinger*'s crew did set the spinnaker and kept it up until the spinnaker boom finally broke in four places. At the turning mark, *Saracen* led *Harbinger* by 35 seconds. *Harbinger* led the third-place boat by four minutes. Then the boats began the long beat back up the North

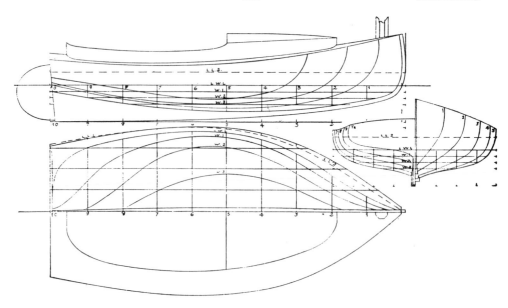

The lines of Harbinger. (Traditions and Memories of American Yachting *by William P. Stephens)*

Shore, cleaving heavy seas past Boston, Nahant, and Swampscott. In the rough going, the owner of a 40-footer was swept overboard and very nearly drowned.

Of the five boats racing with *Harbinger*, one sprung her masthead and needed to be towed home. Another dropped out. *Harbinger* and *Kathleen* both caught and passed *Saracen* in seas now described as "the heaviest of the day." By then, the yachts were approaching Tinker's Island, just off Marblehead Neck. *Harbinger*'s master, taking advantage of his boat's shallow draft, which had apparently *not* hampered her windward performance, cut right inside Tinker's, sailing between the island and the neck. The cutters could not follow. *Harbinger* won the race on both elapsed and corrected time, the latter by some 20 minutes.

In an era when sailors and designers fiercely debated the merits of keel boats versus centerboarders and sloops versus cutters, and whether catboats had any future in the new world of yacht racing, *Harbinger*'s performance was noted by apparently everybody who heard about it or witnessed it. John Hyslop, the expatriate Englishman who installed a ventilating system in the New York Stock Exchange, developed a wave-form theory related to yacht design (independently of the one devised by Colin Archer), and designed and measured many yachts, had this to say: "The *Minerva* has given us some instruction, certainly, but that Cape boat—her performance is something extraordinary." W.P. Stephens wrote that, when the famous cutters "were defeated by an unknown craft, interest shifted to the new type."

Harbinger's performance seemed to contradict all that was then new and modern about sailboat design. "Under such conditions of wind and water," wrote an observer, "the two keel cracks should, if modern theories are correct, have soaked out to windward 3 feet to her 2. . . . Did the *Harbinger* really show as good ability to windward as her two rivals, and if so, how do the experts account for it? Was it her board or her beam or her small displacement or her rig, or all combined, or what?"

Perhaps only C.C. Hanley could have answered that question, but he was keeping his secrets to himself. He calmly set about building a 26-foot catboat with an underhung rudder, 12-foot beam, and 2½-foot draft. This boat he named *Almira*, and in July 1890, she proved herself even *faster* than *Harbinger*. Marine photographer Nathaniel Stebbins, who photographed many Hanley-built boats for their wealthy owners, took pictures of a race between *Almira* and *Harbinger* held on a hot day off South Boston.

Stebbins's photo shows both boats running dead downwind in light air, flying their big spinnakers. *Almira* is ahead by several boat lengths, just where Hanley intended her to be. A crewman aboard *Harbinger* peers forward, perhaps in some disbelief. In an era when purses often went to the winner of sailboat races, Hanley pocketed $250 for this victory and sailed home sustained by a bottle of rum and a

As though she were a knockabout cruiser, the great Harbinger *slices along with a casual air, towing a dinghy. The 28½-footer was launched by C.C. Hanley in 1889. Mast, 40 feet; boom, 40 feet; gaff, 28 feet; hoist, 24 feet; bowsprit, 16 feet. A boat of immense power and racing success until her mast was replaced in 1896. (Henry Peabody photo. Courtesy of The Society for the Preservation of New England Antiquities)*

loaf of bread. *Almira* was still dominating other boats in Massachusetts Bay a quarter of a century later.

Even at the time, both *Harbinger* and *Almira* must have seemed to everyone to be tough acts to follow. Foot for foot, pound for pound, *Almira* may have been the finest racing catboat Hanley ever built. Yet, in the winter of 1896-97, he prepared yet another grand gesture. This was *Thordis*. At 33 feet 4 inches, *Thordis* was longer than her two great predecessors, and at 11 feet 3 inches, proportionally less beamy. Yet she was still of very shallow draft, two feet with the board up. She carried less ballast, too. In 1897, *Thordis* started 17 races and won all of them, defeating, among others, Hanley sloops of comparable size.

What all these racing wins and all the fine boats meant to Charles Hanley was, among other things, money and fame. His clientele was wealthy, for nobody but the wealthy could afford his boats, so Hanley became accustomed to "hobnobbing," as one newspaper said, with influential, wealthy men. In the early 1890s, he built— or caused to be built—a sprawling Victorian-style house in Monument Beach, not far from the summer residence of President Grover Cleveland. In 1898, Cleveland's three daughters were photographed on the comfortable porch of Hanley's house, where they were visiting with his wife, Deborah, and daughter Saidee.

By the mid-1890s, Hanley employed a small workforce—nine men gathered for a group portrait in 1895 or 1896—and operated a blacksmith shop where he created much of the hardware he needed. He had developed many devices to aid in the production of his yachts, although he never bothered to patent any of them. At age 46, Hanley seemed to have arrived. Despite his lack of formal training and his instinctive method of yacht design in an era increasingly given to scientific thinking by educated naval architects, Hanley more than held his own. Then, in 1897, his shop burned down. C.C. was lucky to save the old box of tools given him by his father.

The cause of this fire and the precise reasons why Hanley reacted as he did are unlikely ever to be discovered. Although a press announcement noted Hanley would rebuild in Monument Beach, he never did. He moved to Quincy and built a new shop there instead. When it was ready, he immediately built two sloop-rigged versions of *Thordis*, an enlarged 42-foot version for a Chicago millionaire that allegedly never lost a race, and the famous *Genesee*.

Then Hanley encountered a run of very bad luck indeed. He designed and built four boats for a new 25-foot class adopted by the Massachusetts Yacht Racing Association. Two others were built to class rules by Crowninshield. When it was found that Hanley's boats fell short of meeting the rules by something like an inch of draft, they were disallowed. They had to race among themselves and were known as "Hanley's Orphans." Then he lost out to Bowdoin Crowninshield in the design competition for an America's Cup boat for the 1901 race. He designed a 90-foot centerboarder with a 36-foot beam.

"In the smaller boats, the centerboard types behave well in rough weather and I don't see why a 90-footer should have any greater difficulty," he said.

But the syndicate went for Crowninshield's design, built at Lawley's yard. Crowninshield's boat was *Independence*. She drew 20 feet of water, broke her steering gear on her first two shakedown sails, and had her bottom forced inward on the tow from Boston down to Newport. Later, it was learned that her deep keel had been placed too far back for proper balance. Three months after launching, she was hauled out and broken up. Nat Herreshoff's *Columbia* successfully defended the Cup. Hanley viewed the entire episode with dismay, believing he had lost "the chance of my life."

He also lost his wife, Deborah. She never moved with him to Quincy, and when Hanley did return to Monument Beach, it was to visit his daughter, who had become a teacher. Beginning in 1899, he lived in Quincy with a housekeeper named Susan Smyth, whom he made his heir.

Hanley never built an America's Cup boat because he did not have enough money to do the first-class job he knew was necessary. Some $40,000 had been subscribed for his design, but $75,000 was needed. Perhaps it was to gain a source of greater capital for a future effort that Hanley took on a partner, the wealthy Lorenzo Baker, president of the Standard Fruit Company. Together, they formed the Hanley Construction Company, with Baker as president and Hanley as chief designer. One of the first commissions was another Canada's Cup boat, the 49-foot *Cadillac*, as impeccably finished as all Hanley's boats. *Cadillac* defeated a Crowninshield design to become defender of the Canada's Cup in 1901.

Whatever hopes Hanley had for his partnership with Baker never materialized. "It just didn't work out," said C.W. Garey, who knew Hanley well enough to taste some of the liquor the old builder brewed in his basement. Hanley quit the partnership, then in receivership, in 1903. What he salvaged from the disaster was his tool chest. In January 1904, *The Boston Sunday Herald* published an article about Hanley, a portrait of the boatbuilder as a 53-year-old man down on his luck.

"It was many months after leaving the Construction Company before Mr. Hanley could make up his mind to begin life again at the bottom of the ladder, although he was down to his last dollar, and already knew what want was. He is now willing to admit that there were days, a year ago, that he was very hungry, but was successful in concealing this fact from his friends."

Even had friends recognized his plight, it is doubtful that they would have been particularly worried. "Some of his old admirers," said the *Herald*, "had declared that if ever left on a barren island, the only person they would wish for would be Hanley, because he could do much with nothing."

Except for his tools, Hanley had, in fact, almost nothing. He had pretty much decided to give up on boatbuilding when he received a letter asking him to design and build a 25-foot sloop. With that, Hanley began to take an interest in life again. He received some offers of capital to start a new company, but these he turned down. He used his reputation and the sloop order to borrow money. With the money, he bought two acres in Germantown, just across the Town River from the Hanley Construction Company.

There Hanley built a small hut in which to live while he built his new shop. He did not have enough money to pay the town for water service, so he bought a pump and dug a well of his own. He laid the keel for the sloop, and when spring came, he moved into a tent on the riverbank. When he finished the boat, he had enough money to begin building another house, much less grand than the one in Monument Beach but trimmed in hardwoods and put together as well as any of his boats. He did most of the work by himself, then built another boat and put an addition onto his shop, sawing the timbers and fabricating all the hardware on the spot.

Hanley expanded this yard gradually, over a number of years. He remained an outgoing man who was known to enjoy alcohol, either alone or with friends, and, during Prohibition, he turned his inventive mind to ensuring that he did not want for his daily drinks. In his later middle age, he looked much like those ruddy portraits one associates with Santa Claus, possessed of the same bushy eyebrows but without the beard. Then, one September night in 1920, Hanley's boatyard was enveloped by an enormous fire that attracted thousands of onlookers and consumed every building Hanley had erected, including his house.

Said a local paper, "The morning after the fire, he walked about the ruins of his yard, stroking and patting the sides of the yachts which were spared by the flames and talking to them as if they were things alive, as they were to Captain Hanley. . . . It was enough to discourage the ordinary man, but Mr. Hanley never knew such a word as failure."

He rebuilt the yard as best he could, and in 1925, sold it to his neighbor, Fred Lawley. After that, C.C. concentrated on gardening and a basement distillery in which he made, according to all who tasted it, some very fine rum. When journalists visited, they came away referring to the old boatbuilder as "living in hard earned retirement" and usually called him "a merry old boy."

Hanley had become a kind of legend in Quincy. It was often said that any right-minded Quincy boy had no higher aspiration than to own a Hanley catboat. He never built any more boats after he retired, but with the help of a talented Norwegian draftsman named Erland Debes, who worked at the Fall River Shipyard in Quincy and had often tended *Almira*'s mainsheet, he published a design brochure. The brochure included five catboats, from 16½ to 35 feet, a knockabout sloop, and a runabout. Later, he and Debes designed a boat for George Sheahan, Hanley's physician, whose brother, Henry Beston Sheahan, wrote the Cape Cod classic, *The Outermost House*.

Sheahan wanted a cruising boat, and Hanley presented him with the design for a 28-foot cat-rigged yawl with an 11-foot 9-inch beam and a board-up draft of 2 feet 6 inches. Board down, the boat drew 6 feet 9 inches. The mainmast was a bit farther aft than one might expect to find it, so there would be more room to handle the anchor and less strain on the bow.

They "kept her light and as yachty as possible, seeking to avoid the monster type of catboat," reported Sheahan in 1928. "The cat yawl has proved a good one, the advantages being mainly the absence of backstays and having the mainsail inboard. As foretold by Hanley, the little jigger acts as a wonderful weather vane in breezy weather." The doctor named his boat for his two daughters, calling her *Two Sisters*. She was built in 1927 by what was then called the Baker Yacht Basin, located on the site where Hanley had built his first yard in Quincy many years earlier.

Doctor Sheahan visited the yard frequently. "It was a pleasant experience," he wrote later, "for there's no better fun than to see your boat come into being unless like Joshua Slocum and Harry Pidgeon you build her yourself."

Together with an ex-whaling skipper friend, his brother Henry, Debes, and an old rigger, Sheahan regularly cruised *Two Sisters* from Quincy to Annisquam or down to Cape Cod and south, waters he called the "South Seas of New England." He wrote about his cruises, from time to time, for yachting periodicals.

After *Two Sisters* was complete, Hanley's design career apparently ceased for

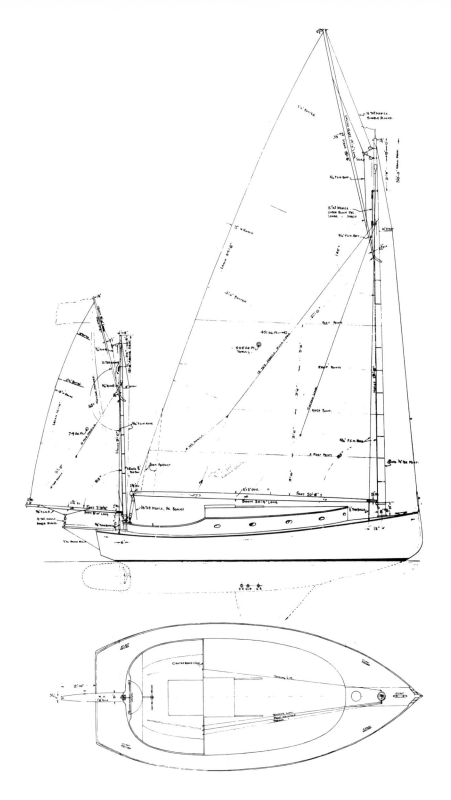

Sail and deck plans for Two Sisters *as drawn by Erland Debes in 1927. (Courtesy Paul and Mollie Birdsall)*

good. He was in his late 70s then and was recognized for his many achievements. Just before he died, M.I.T.'s famous professor of naval architecture, George Owen, accepted three of Hanley's half-models. These were his famous Canada's Cup sloop *Genesee*, the decked racing catboat *Cleopatra*—built for Melbourne MacDowell, husband of the actress Fanny Davenport, and named for her greatest character—and *Mucilage*.

C.C. Hanley died on July 4, 1934. Professor Owen said of C.C. that he "had a genius in proportion which makes him worthy to rank among the greatest leaders in the development of racing yachts." Nathanael Herreshoff, his great rival, had this to say: "Captain Hanley was the hardest nut I had to crack."

Two Sisters, now *Mollie B.*, was not the first catboat owned by the Birdsalls. They bought *Sally*, a 21-foot Crosby-built boat, in 1953, nine months after they were married.

"She was," said Mollie, "our first child."

They discovered the boat one winter day when they went for a walk. Tacked to a sign outside the Middletown, Connecticut, yacht club was a notice that a catboat was for sale. Mollie memorized the phone number and they called later that day. The boat, they learned, needed work. Most of the keel was rotten and the centerboard trunk was going, too. The decks needed to be replaced. None of this stopped Paul Birdsall. He had spent summers on Nantucket when there were still many catboats there, and he had worked for a man who rented party boats. He got so he could sail a catboat in and out of the wharves at the town waterfront.

The Birdsalls decided to buy *Sally* despite her ills, and Paul went to the bank to withdraw the money he had saved from his army paychecks. At a time when young couples were expected to buy a house and have babies, the Birdsalls bought an old catboat.

"People thought we were out of our minds," said Mollie.

The Birdsalls made the necessary repairs to the boat and added accommodations for the children they soon produced, much to the relief of their neighbors. Still, some were dismayed when they began taking the infants sailing.

"They'd cluck their tongues," Mollie remembers. "People were really shocked. This was before anybody did things with their babies or children."

The Birdsalls did things. Each year, they spent between 50 to 80 days aboard with their sons, a pair of Welsh corgis, and even an occasional relative or friend. They entered the boat in the Off Soundings races and did reasonably well, especially when the wind blew hard enough to require a single reef. Occasionally, after placing among the top three in her class, *Sally* would have to carry a substantial penalty, but this did nothing to dampen the Birdsalls' enthusiasm for the races, which they attended for 15 years. Once each year, they attended a race for catboats at Duck Island, Connecticut, out of which was formed The Catboat Association with Paul as a cofounder and Mollie as treasurer. They cruised Long Island Sound, Cape Cod, and Nantucket and, as quiet, uncrowded anchorages became ever more difficult to find, began looking curiously at charts of the Maine coast. That was when they decided they needed a larger boat.

"The long passages," said Mollie, "just took a *long* time."

Being a cofounder of The Catboat Association had its advantages when it came

Paul and Mollie Birdsall aboard their cat yawl. (Stan Grayson photo)

to boat buying. One day, Paul received a "boat for sale" ad intended for *The Catboat Association Bulletin*, which John Leavens had begun to publish. Instead of passing along the ad, Paul went down to see the boat himself. She was then in the hands of her third owner, had a reputation as a leaker, and needed work. The Birdsalls bought the boat at once.

They began stripping varnish with the idea of redoing the brightwork, but soon decided to paint the wood instead. More important, they refastened the boat, discovering in the process that the garboards had pulled slightly away from the keel. They hired a boatbuilder to repair the planks. He drove wedges into the centerboard slot to widen it and ensured that the slot could not close by bolting bronze angles through the keel and the new floor timbers. Paul did all the refastening himself. In the first winter, he completed the bottom, and in the second winter, the topsides. He discovered 1,000 pounds of lead embedded in the boat's skeg, the reason *Mollie B.* carried so little inside ballast and had such a seakindly motion. Repairs complete, *Mollie B.* could be sailed hard. She did not leak anymore. The Birdsalls began making trips to Maine. In 1971, they sailed from Connecticut to Monhegan, homing on the RDF transmitter on Manana, in less than 48 hours.

"We noticed a tremendous difference once we had the new boat," said Paul, "in terms of how much less fatigued we were, because there was more room to move around and because we were more comfortable in port. We learned, too, that she is definitely a faster model than *Sally* and sails fantastically well, although she is not especially weatherly."

Double-reefed, the cat yawl often averaged six to seven knots, and, particularly after the addition of a small jib, she proved handy and well balanced. The jib, which came from an old Wianno Senior, had been discovered by Wilton Crosby, Jr. being used as a drop cloth in the paint shop.

By the time the Birdsalls completed their 1971 cruise to Maine, they knew they had what was, for them, the perfect boat. They stored *Mollie B.* away in the boatyard for the winter, already thinking ahead to the next year's cruise. Then, one day in March, the spark from a workman's electrical tool started a fire in a huge boat-storage shed. The flames spread fast, curling up the ropes leading to dust covers above the boats and enveloping the tarps and everything that was beneath them. Fuel tanks ruptured and added to the fire. Inside the shed, rows of powerboats and motorsailers, many with gasoline still in their tanks, were incinerated.

As the fires blazed higher, gasoline and diesel fuel ran out of ruptured tanks. It trickled out along the shed's wall, and the fire licked eagerly along its path to the line of boats stored outside the shed, six or eight feet away from the wall. That is where the fire found *Mollie B.* Before firefighters could stop it, the fire had scorched the hull and destroyed the rails, decks, and much of the cabintop and sides. It consumed a fine new rudder built of quarter-sawn oak. The firefighters were able to do more for *Mollie B.* than for many other boats, but, in the end, when the fires were quenched and the boatyard was a sodden, ashen place of ruin, the old yawl was declared a total loss. It was as if the flames that dogged C.C. Hanley for all his life had risen up to claim his last showpiece.

"We had increased our insurance coverage," said Paul of the disaster, "but it still was not high enough to cover the eight or nine thousand it would have cost to have a yard rebuild the boat." He bought back the wreck for $300, and together with a friend, went to work on *Mollie B.* all over again.

They replaced all the decking except for one part right aft that was undamaged. They rebuilt the cabin sides and cockpit coamings using several layers of marine plywood. They built a new cabintop. Then they fiberglassed the cabin and decks. They made new rails, and all the time they worked, they feared *another* fire.

"The salvage crew that descended on the yard," said Paul, "was a very fly-by-night operation, careless. They were using special chainsaws to cut metal with, and a lot of the tanks in the hulks still contained fuel and little fires were starting. Finally, the salvage crew got fed up and left and never paid the yard owner what they owed."

Paul and his friend labored on. They replaced *Mollie B.*'s Gray gasoline engine with a 25-horsepower Westerbeke diesel. They placed a few dutchmen in the bottom planking where it was severely scorched. In two months of almost nonstop effort, the boat was ready for launching. Paul and his friend spent the first night afloat on board. For company they had a big pump and a bottle of good bourbon.

Although I sailed with the Birdsalls in mid-September, and Paul had already seen a hint of frost on Blue Hill, the day was more like summer, more like August. By the

The Mollie B. *off Block Island. This photograph was taken three months after a boatyard fire nearly destroyed her. (Saybrook Studio photo. Courtesy Paul and Mollie Birdsall)*

time we left Joel White's boatyard, the wind was light and variable, puffing softly first from the southwest, then the southeast. We powered away from the moorings, past the little green Friendship sloop White had built for his father, and out between two rock ledges into island-strewn Penobscot Bay.

Mollie B. was well equipped, her gear well stowed. On the foredeck, she carried a Danforth and a yachtsman anchor. The diesel hummed smoothly.

"Going to sea in a boat," said Paul, "you don't go with things a mess. It's like going into the woods in wintertime with horses. If you get blocked in and can't turn around, you need to have the right equipment. So I carry a chain saw, axe, and peavey. So if I do get hung up someplace, I can free myself."

After working with horses for years, he has come to see many similarities between them and catboats, similarities he tends to describe in terms of honesty of design and purpose, lack of pretense. Now, he also tends to talk to various components of his boat as if he were directing a horse. "Board down." "Engine forward." We might have been borne to sea atop the broad back of a patient Belgian draft horse. *Mollie B.*, 54 years old, ran easily up Eggemoggin Reach under main, mizzen, and jib. There was a nice precision to the way she steered, and despite the lightness of the breeze, the boat was enjoyable to sail.

After a while, Mollie and the apprentices got out some lunch, and Paul told about the time his boat had almost been wrecked. She was 10 years old then. "Doctor Sheahan," he said, "had a cottage in a cove on Quincy Bay. He kept *Two Sisters* there, moored. One summer—it was the summer of 1938—a neighbor moved a swimming raft into the cove, and Sheahan complained to himself and his family that this *thing*, this *raft*, was in the way of his mooring. Then the hurricane of 1938 bowled into the bay and *Two Sisters* began to drag fast toward shore. She dragged and she dragged and she would have gone right on dragging 'til she hit the rocks. But she did not. She fouled the swimming raft. The swimming raft saved her." He had been told the story *personally* by one of the two sisters herself, when she was an older woman.

Off Green Island Light, we jibed softly and bore in toward Blue Hill. We sailed past Long Island, where the spruce trees clustered thick and white granite poked up from beneath the soil, here and there, like the ribs and spine of the earth. The sun shone above us like a bright new penny as we coasted on down east, the apprentices now sunning themselves atop the cabin. We might have been sailing across some glossy postcard of Maine in summer. When the wind shifted directly astern, we winged out the little jib and the mizzen and looked back at our smooth wake. Then it seemed, if we could but listen hard enough, we would hear the spirit of old C.C., chuckling delightedly to himself in the dark water of our wake.

11

A Cruise in Momcat

IN JULY OF 1982, Doris Johnson, editor of *The Catboat Association Bulletin* and owner of a 20-foot wooden catboat, invited me to sail with her to Martha's Vineyard for an Association race and rendezvous to be held at Oak Bluffs. I arrived at Doris's home in Kingston, Massachusetts, the evening before to help with final preparations. Doris was not there at the time, being occupied with assorted errands, but I was greeted by several cats and the sight of an old fiberglass dinghy resting on a layer of newspapers in the family room. There Doris had been at work, tending to the boat's several needs. She had cleaned it up, mended its rubber rubrails and, in her well-equipped workshop, fashioned two pieces of oak with which to make new mounts for the oarlocks. While Doris finished her errands, I began drilling the holes necessary to install the mounts, and when she returned, we bored larger holes so that the sockets could be set into the mounts.

When this and other jobs were done, we put the dinghy and supplies into Doris's station wagon and drove to Duxbury, where *Momcat* lay like a turtle on the mud beside a dock at Long Point Marine. There, earlier that day, the engine's defunct generator had been replaced by a new alternator. No longer would Doris need to wonder whether the ammeter was hooked up backward "because the needle always points to discharge." We returned to the boat shortly before five o'clock the next morning, an hour at which the tide would serve to make an easy passage out of Duxbury Bay while leaving us adequate time to catch a fair tide at both the Cape Cod Canal and Woods Hole.

It was not a promising morning. The sky exhibited a variety of colors, all of them

145

shades of gray, and the only creature we spotted besides ourselves was a gull. The bird sat atop a piling facing into a stiff northeast breeze. What with the weather and the heavy layer of dew on *Momcat*'s buff-yellow topsides, we put on our foul-weather gear. With the metallic clatter of the Red Wing's starter, the gull flew off. We dropped our docklines and, a few minutes later, were motoring along on a course that took us past the monument to Myles Standish and toward the squat lighthouse that local sailors call "Bug Light." Ahead was Cape Cod Bay.

Approaching the bay, we raised sail and made our way to the buoy from which we would turn south on our course to the mouth of the canal. Since the course provided us with a reach, we decided to shut down the engine and sail for a time, checking our progress to make sure we'd arrive in time to have a fair tide through to Buzzards Bay. The wind was blowing some 15 to 18 knots, and all around us were dark black-green seas capped with silver. There was enough wind for *Momcat* to show some weather helm, and it was a struggle, sometimes, to keep on our compass course and not be lifted away to the east.

It was not the most promising seascape I had ever seen, but Doris was entirely unconcerned. She went below and undertook a job she had long been detoured from, much to her frustration. She began removing the two wooden "fiddles" from the midsection of *Momcat*'s centerboard-mounted table. These two wooden strips were placed precisely so as *not* to allow a cup or 12-ounce can to rest between them. Unfortunately, not long after Doris began what was, in fact, a delicate job, we were lifted by a wave; the tool she was working with slipped and one fiddle broke.

"I looked out," she told me later, "and saw another wave coming in on the quarter and it was higher than your head."

She set aside her job for a calmer time and came back topside. Because it was gusting somewhat more strongly than before and it was now more difficult to keep on our course, we started the engine and motorsailed our way toward Sandwich and the canal. The motorsailing began uneventfully enough, and Doris was quietly telling me about the time, shortly after she acquired *Momcat*, that the mast cracked, when she happened to look at the oil pressure gauge.

"The oil pressure seems to be going down," she said.

Sure enough, instead of pointing at 40 on the dial, the white needle was wavering between 30 and 35 pounds. The gauge was being as contrary as her ammeter had been. We lifted the hatch over the engine and looked down into the bilge. There, sure enough, was all the oil that should have been circulating through the Red Wing and keeping the white needle in the center of the dial. I asked Doris if she had more oil, and she promptly produced a quart, which we used to refill the sump. The needle returned to indicate normal oil pressure. There was no visible leak. We continued on, Doris telling me how the mast, which she had believed to have been made of solid spruce, was found to be fir in its lower section. She made this discovery in a difficult way; the mast broke at the place where the fir and spruce were joined. When that happened, the stick was removed from the boat and a piece of spruce was scarfed to the upper two-thirds. Doris's concern with the mast *this* season involved the wedges. They did not seem sufficient to keep the spar from rotating somewhat when tacking or jibing, and nothing she did, no amount of hammering or rewedging, seemed to help.

We were discussing the sad absence of literature on mast wedges when the oil pressure began dropping again. We opened the engine hatch, and sure enough, there was more oil in the bilge.

"I just got those bilges good and clean," Doris said.

Since the Red Wing was running well and there was no hint of oil in the exhaust, it was clear that we were leaking oil rather than burning it. In fact, the amount of oil now glistening atop *Momcat*'s bilge planking suggested we were losing oil at an alarming rate. I reached down and explored the oil pan with my fingers, meanwhile wondering what I would do if there *was* a hole down there. Was there wood aboard from which to whittle a plug? I remembered a motor-pool sergeant in Vietnam who claimed he once repaired the holed sump of a jeep with "a plug made of bacon."

But I could find no hole in the sump. I lay down on the cockpit sole and examined the engine as closely as I could. No revelations. I wiped off every trace of oil from its red-painted crankcase and then stared at it, hoping to find a small, telltale, emergent streak. There were no streaks. The oil pressure continued to fall. Why was it, I wondered aloud, that there always seemed to be *something*. Our well-planned timetable and hopes for an enjoyable passage faded with each decline of the oil pressure gauge. After a few minutes with my head in the bilge, the boat rising and falling, I knew I'd had enough. I got up and stood in the companionway, staring off at the dark gray line that was Cape Cod.

"Are you OK?" Doris asked.

"I am," I answered, fighting the onset of the queasies, "but I've had enough of that for now. I didn't see anything wrong."

There were two quarts of oil remaining, and as we approached the stone jetty at the east end of the canal, we emptied one of them into the engine. By the time we were a third of the way through the canal, the oil pressure was down to 12 pounds, and I emptied the last quart into the oil filler tube. Even the passage east of the big schooner *Pride of Baltimore*, with her rakish masts and big ensign, did nothing to lessen the anxiety I now felt. We had slowed the engine, hoping to reduce the rate at which its life blood was being pumped into the bottom of the boat, but the slower we went, the more likely it became that the tide would turn before we had completed our passage through the canal. The wind, what was left of it, was now right on our bow. In the smooth water of the canal, I again examined the engine for a leak, but could find none.

The tide began to turn before we reached the Bourne Bridge, and by then, the oil pressure was down to 12 pounds again and falling. Now we needed more throttle to make any headway. By the time we neared the bridge, the current was running strong against us; we were making little progress and the oil pressure was about 10 pounds. We decided to pull in to the Corps of Engineers docks just beyond the bridge and, shepherded there by the corps' patrol boat *Wampanoag*, we did. The currents rushed through the looming steel docks, and *Momcat* seemed suddenly fragile, egglike among them as we made our harried landfall and, with great relief, shut down the engine. Out of nowhere, an observer appeared.

"You can't go through the canal against the current," he advised. "You looked like you were about to go backward."

"Engine trouble," I said, without looking at him. He took the hint and went away.

We discussed what to do. We had barely begun our cruise and were faced with the possibility of having to end it because of serious engine trouble. "If this were a two-cycle engine, we wouldn't have this problem," I offered, "because it wouldn't have a sump or any oil to put in it."

"Didn't things used to happen to them anyway?" Doris asked.

"Well, of course something could go wrong. . . ."

Just in case we really were faced with something dreadful, it seemed advisable to see if there was a marina berth nearby. We decided I would walk into Bourne, buy some oil and sodas, and call a marina. Doris did not like the marina idea and was not backward about letting me know it. The idea of seeking the advice of a professional mechanic to solve a problem most likely created by another professional mechanic did not enthuse her.

"I want Oscar Pease," she said plaintively. "He'll know what to do." She began talking about waiting for the tide to turn and then *sailing* all the way to Martha's Vineyard. "We could just use the engine for that little bit at Woods Hole."

I stepped ashore and began the short walk into Bourne.

"While you're gone, I'll make lunch," Doris said.

Disappointed that we had had no success at all in locating the source of trouble with the 20-year-old engine, I left her in the cockpit, unwrapping bread.

In 1895, a year before he left Osterville to set up shop in Brooklyn, Manley Crosby built two catboats destined to have a particularly lasting impact upon our understanding of the type. This was because lines for both, not to mention lines for two earlier designs by Horace Crosby, were published in Howard Chapelle's *American Sailing Craft*. It was a book of immediate and long-lasting interest to anyone involved seriously with traditional boats, and boat enthusiasts and builders throughout the country eventually bought or borrowed the book. Chapelle (who spoke to The Catboat Association at its annual meeting in Mystic in 1964) summed up Manley's two boats in his book. These boats, he said, "may be taken as examples of modern Cape Cod cats, as there has been practically no change in hull form since their time. The addition of a motor made no difference in their form, as the deadwood needed only to be cut for the propeller aperture. The motor is usually located under a box in the cockpit."

One of those who read Chapelle's book was a Duxbury boatbuilder named Gordon Tucker. He already owned a 24-foot Manley Crosby catboat, but he was fascinated by the lines he saw in *American Sailing Craft*. Because he found his boat too large and heavy, he decided to adapt the published lines to a smaller boat.

"I took the basic waterline and reduced it to about 20 feet," he said, "and then I stirred in a few ideas of mine since you don't just take a big boat and make an exact but smaller duplicate. You might give it a little more freeboard and beam in relation to its length, for instance."

In the spare time he had left over from building small rowboats, sailboats, and outboard-powered craft, he began construction of the catboat one winter during the late 1950s. He did not do anything he called "fancy" during construction. "It has average workboat construction," he said, "as catboats originally had." But he used the finest materials. The keel and frames were oak and the planks were Philippine mahogany fastened with bronze screws. He found the rig, which came from a catboat of some 20 feet in Edgartown, hanging in an old-timer's basement, and bought it for 50 dollars. It lasted 10 years, until a day he went out without

Doris Johnson aboard Momcat.

reefing in a good breeze and the mast broke at the deck. Tucker then discovered a large, brittle knot buried in the wood there. As construction continued, he bought an old four-cylinder, 17 horsepower Red Wing engine and rebuilt it using parts obtained from a man who had purchased all the spare parts when the Minnesota manufacturer ceased production. By the time Tucker was through with it, the Red Wing was essentially brand-new.

Although he had always wanted to cruise his catboat throughout New England, Gordon Tucker never left the immediate area of Duxbury Bay. There he daysailed the boat for some 20 years before he decided to sell it and concentrate on a new gaff-rigged sloop he was completing. At the same time he made this decision, Doris Johnson decided it was time for her to buy a new sailboat. She settled on finding a catboat because she had always liked their looks and sailing characteristics and because, although she had several children, she could not count on them to want to go sailing.

"Whatever I bought," she said, "I had to be able to sail by myself."

She began her search in Quincy, where she works as a newspaper reporter, and explored boatyards all along the 30 miles of shore between office and home. Each day, she stopped off at another yard. She found some catboats for sale but the prices were always too high. One day, she decided to visit Long Point Marine in Duxbury and ask the owner, Dwight Smith, if he knew of anything available.

"I walked down to the dock and there was this pretty little boat, sitting there, freshly painted, with no name on the transom, and I thought it was either for sale or the owner just had never named it. I thought, 'I *want* this.'" She recognized the boat as one she had long admired. She was impressed with its workmanship and its small, but, for her, ample cabin. It was July 4, and there was nobody at the yard. She returned the next day and told the owner, a fellow Kingston resident and friend, "I *want* that boat."

"How did you know it was for sale?" he asked.

"I didn't," she replied, shocked. "I've seen her on her mooring in the Bluefish River for years. But I had no idea she was for sale."

"Well it is," he told her, "because the man who built her is almost done with a new sloop."

She bought the boat in 1979 and her children settled on its first name ever— *Momcat*. She affixed the letters to the graceful transom herself.

By the time I got back to the boat with an armful of quart oilcans and sodas, Doris had produced a variety of sandwiches, each one tasting better than the other. When lunch was complete, the sun was, for the first time that day, shining brightly, and Doris again began talking about continuing our trip despite the engine's problems. We could still, she believed, make Woods Hole in time to catch the tide, using the engine just enough to help us through. Then, when we got to the Vineyard, Oscar could have a look. Everything would yet be fine. This idea had so much more appeal than tying up in Bourne and spending the weekend repairing the engine that I agreed.

We soon had the boat ready and, with the sump full once again, caught the tide going out of the canal. We emerged into Buzzards Bay and found a sparkling millpond with an obliging northerly of eight or 10 knots to push us along. And it was there, in the smooth waters of the bay, that I finally found the oil leak. Before we left the docks, we had cleaned off the engine completely, using most of Doris's paper towels in the process. Then, with no danger of getting seasick, I cozied up to it again and stared. Gradually, from what should have been the most obvious yet was in fact the least obvious place, the oil began to flow in a golden trickle. Oil was coming out all around a bolt that attached the new alternator. The bolt, barely accessible, ran right through a section of the oil system, but it had never been tightened. I could rotate it with my fingers. Because of the bolt's location, it took several minutes with wrench and screwdriver before it was tightened down. After that, no more oil leaked out and the gauge once again registered a comforting, unwavering 40 pounds.

We shut the engine off and continued our run down Buzzards Bay, past Cleveland Ledge where the onetime president used to fish, and on toward Woods Hole, happy and barely even thinking about all the oil that remained sloshing in the bilge. If our delay at the canal had a benefit, it was this: Our arrival at Woods Hole coincided precisely with slack water. We entered the reef-bordered passage in the early evening beneath a gray sky, and made an easy trip of it out into Vineyard Sound. By now, it had grown chilly again, and we were adding clothing as we reached toward Oak Bluffs. On our port side, over Cape Cod, we could see black clouds hovering, and rain.

It was almost dark when we finally motored slowly into Oak Bluffs to find the harbor crowded with catboats. We rafted up to *Ginger*, an 18-foot Fenwick Williams design owned by Cort and Joanne Schuyler, and absolutely loaded with dozens of clever touches enabling them to range widely.

"One thing," I said, as we rowed the dinghy to the beach. "At least these new oak oarlock mounts work." We chuckled together over the idea that *something* had worked without a glitch.

On the beach, a cookout was in progress. Oscar Pease was moving among the gathering, dispensing some particularly delicious cookies. "Nellie sent these along," he said, holding out a big round tin full of baked goods. Between bites, Doris told him about all the oil in *Momcat*'s bilge. "Get Lemon Joy," he said. "It will emulsify the oil same as anything labeled 'bilge cleaner.' You can wash it right out with the bilge pump. Take another cookie."

It was past midnight when we rowed back to *Momcat* and made up the berths. A certain amount of contortion was involved here. At some point, when Gordon Tucker understood he would only be daysailing instead of cruising, he had reduced the cabin's size, moving the companionway from starboard to the center, and enlarged the cockpit. The boat thus has somewhat less room below than a fiberglass 18-footer, but Doris manages to cruise for as much as two weeks anyhow. To port is the head and a berth, to starboard the propane stove and a berth. Stowed or hanging about are all the little items Doris has, after years of experience, found useful: mirror, hand-bearing compass, a wide variety of snack foods, condiments, a lantern. Time and again I saw Doris pluck anything she needed from one place or another in *Momcat*'s cabin, and she cooked the most memorable of swordfish steaks on the two-burner stove.

"She's got so much gear on the boat now," said Gordon Tucker, "that she could probably take out some ballast. But she's gone far, farther than I ever did."

In fact, Doris has ranged over all the prime cruising grounds from Plymouth to Newport. In doing so, she has developed a high degree of self-sufficiency and is able to confront most any problem that may present itself, be it a 10-hour stint at the wheel, single-reefed in heavy seas, or making and fitting a new, more efficient boom crutch.

With the berths made up, we opened the four bronze ports and the companionway, which Doris covered with an opened beach umbrella, yielding increased ventilation while keeping out the evening dew. I took a last look out. All the boats in Oak Bluffs' little harbor lay still upon the dark water, while in the encircling houses, candle lights flickered and gradually were snuffed out. We'd been up for 18 hours and had experienced the satisfying pleasure that comes from making a successful, self-sufficient passage in a small cruising sailboat. On *Momcat*'s narrow berths, we slept well.

Before 1907, Oak Bluffs was known as Cottage City. It was named for the many brightly decorated wooden cottages built there around a camp meeting ground. Catboat races were held there in those days, too, and one of them, in 1877, was photographed. The photo shows the fleet not far from shore where a crowd has gathered to watch, with the women in long dresses and carrying parasols against the sun, and the gentlemen in top hats.

The cottages still stand at Oak Bluffs, a collection of Victorian finery evocative of dozens of gaily decorated birthday cakes. Catboat racing still takes place there, too. On the morning after our arrival, we made our way to the starting line and soon were tacking back and forth awaiting the gun. There seemed to be at least 35 or 40 other catboats sailing back and forth through the green water, more than in the old photograph, in fact, and the most serious skippers were already bunching up at the windward end of the starting line.

Although Doris had already shown herself to be a resourceful and determined cruising sailor, she now made it clear that she had little use for competition. Competition was not why she went sailing. Such races as this are supposed to be strictly for fun, but there are always those who take them too seriously. From our vantage point to leeward, we could now see the result. A number of big catboats were tacking about, asserting rights to position, and booms were swinging dangerously close to sails and rigging. I wondered what would happen if a 25-foot boom in mid-jibe caught somebody's topping lift.

"Nobody is going to win this race on the starting line, anyway," I said, looking at a copy of the course. It would take us out into Nantucket Sound and back to the island at Vineyard Haven.

"Who cares about winning?" Johnson asked. "We're supposed to be having a good time." She had not minded at all being awarded a little blue ditty bag for finishing *last* in a Duxbury race the previous month.

We stayed well clear of the starting-line confusion and crossed the line well back in the fleet as it ran before a light northwesterly breeze toward the first mark. One of the reasons *Momcat* makes such a good singlehanded cruising boat is that her sail area is not excessive, being some 280 square feet. Thus, she is not a particularly fast boat, but, as long as I had the wheel, I thought I would try to do my very best with her while keeping Doris from noticing. She handled *Momcat* on the run to the mark. In the light air, the wooden boats tended to bunch up and fall behind the lighter, fiberglass versions. This created a turning mark just as crowded as the starting line. There was even some mild bumping, much to Doris's disgust. She gave me the wheel as soon as we had rounded and settled down for the long haul to the gong off West Chop.

Thirteen wooden catboats had started the race, and with two exceptions, they were all still close to *Momcat*. Pulling ahead even then was mighty *Cimba*, an immaculately turned-out Fenwick Williams 25-footer sailed by Frank Cassidy and his wife, Lynda, who is treasurer of The Catboat Association. *Cimba* was followed by *Judy*, a 26-footer built by Daniel Crosby in the 1920s. Owned by a onetime commercial diver named Ned Kelley, *Judy* is renowned for her speed and overall sailing ability. Since both *Cimba* and *Judy* were larger and faster boats than *Momcat* and can be counted upon to finish one-two in most races they enter, I turned my attention to the boats around us. They made an interesting assortment.

Among them was *Trim Again*, a 24-foot Eldredge-McInnis design that had been built by W.W. Phinney's onetime apprentice, Merton Long. There was *Catena*, a 20-foot keel-centerboard catboat designed in the early 1960s by naval architect Walter Skinner, and there were two of Fenwick Williams's 18-footers, the Schuylers' *Ginger* and Bob Mone's *Hannah Screecham*. Close by, too, were *Pinkletink*, the Crosby boat John Leavens had owned for years, now sailed by Ted Lindberg, Sr.; Oscar Pease in *Vanity* with Pinkie Leavens and Leland Brown for crew; *Meta B.*, designed and built by Nathaniel Benjamin, who has a boatshop in Vineyard Haven; *Genevieve*, built by Herbert and Andrew Crosby in the early Thirties; and *Matchless*.

By now the wind was beginning to show signs of strengthening, at the same time

Momcat *snugged down at Wellfleet. (Stan Grayson photo)*

shifting about and occasioning a fairly constant trimming of sails. *Momcat* edged past *Trim Again* and the two 18-footers and then *Vanity*, but I paid little attention when several of the boats began falling off to the northwest, a course taking them well away from the rhumb line to the next mark. At the time, I thought little of this, especially since Oscar Pease had not altered course to follow them.

Midafternoon found us battling the short, steep three-foot seas typical of the sound, our progress impeded further as the wind occasionally took brief coffee breaks. It was not long before we knew something was going on, and Doris quickly determined what it was. She hauled out her tide tables and we saw, quite graphically, that we were struggling against a turned tide in an area where the velocity is greatest. Had we been cruising, Doris doubtless would have checked for tidal currents. Since we were racing, she had not. Now, looking back at Oscar aboard *Vanity*, I saw it all clearly. If there was one person in the world who would care less about winning a race than Doris Johnson, it was Oscar Pease.

We now began the discouraging series of tacks necessary to get us to the red gong, tilting steeply in the current. We were still occupied thusly when the first of the boats we had passed earlier, taking advantage of the tide, made the mark and sailed off toward the distant finish line. We made it eventually, too, of course, and *Momcat*'s eighth-place finish out of the 13 wooden boats elicited a number of congratulations. Overall honors went to a Marshall 22 from Nantucket that apparently *flew* around the course in just over 1¾ hours, some 12 minutes ahead of *Cimba*.

That evening, the bridge tender at Vineyard Haven opened the main-road drawbridge that gives access to Lagoon Pond, and, one by one, some two dozen catboats entered the pond and slowly cruised the two miles to its head. Doris snapped pictures of the fleet, several of which later appeared in *The Catboat Association Bulletin*, as, all around us, cameras clicked and crews shouted impressions of the afternoon. We anchored in some six feet of water at the very head of Lagoon Pond, a quiet place bordered by trees and salt marsh.

By dinnertime, a fire was going and steaks and burgers were cooking on the grill. John Leavens had arrived from his house on a Chilmark knoll. He was sitting in a garden chair on the pebbly beach, and catboaters, trying not to monopolize him, were taking turns sitting in the empty chair next to him and reminiscing about the Association, its people and catboats.

"Catboats, catboats," Leavens said. "If it's got to do with catboats, I want to know about it." He looked around at the gathering. "Isn't this something," he said. "Who'd have thought, when we started the Association, that it would ever turn into something like this?"

He stayed until the flooding tide began to threaten not only the fire but his chair, and then went home with Pinkie. Now the clear summer sky was peppered with bright stars and the anchored boats lay without movement on the dark pond. Walking down the beach to make sure our dinghy was pulled up high enough and would not drift away, I heard a voice, vaguely familiar, and saw a couple pushing off in their own dinghy. Their dark figures made barely a silhouette against the water.

"You know," the man was saying, "this is what it could have looked like around here, a hundred years ago."

And then I remembered. It was the same man I'd heard three years earlier, voicing the same sentiment, at Townsend Hornor's rendezvous in Osterville. In a moment he had disappeared, and there was only the gentle squeak of his oars, working in the locks, and his wife's voice answering.

"There's something about this all," she was saying, "that's a comfort."

Appendix:
On Myths
and the Sailing of Catboats

ONCE, WHEN HE WAS a member of a panel on catboat sailing techniques at an Association meeting in Mystic, Ned Kelley, skipper of the 26-foot Daniel Crosby catboat *Judy*, remarked that "catboat sailing is almost like windsurfing. It's totally different from any other kind of sailing you're used to."

This may, at first glance, seem to be an overstatement, but a modest book could be written about the subject, discussing everything from the comparative merits of attaching the sail to the mast with lacelines or mast hoops (lines can allow the luff to take a fuller curve and may reduce the potential for hang-ups when hoisting and lowering sail) to heaving-to and reefing. In fact, The Catboat Association has compiled a booklet on catboat sailing techniques.

Even very good sailors may be dumbfounded by their first exposure to a catboat. Most approach the boats with the quite proper notion that they are comparatively simple without understanding the various subtleties imposed by that simplicity. The big sail is always daunting, and there often seems to be a peculiar insensitivity to the fact that the sail is going to require some different attitudes toward sailing and seamanship.

"I thought catboats were supposed to be simple," the former owner of a 30-foot keel sloop once told me. "This is harder than my other boat."

We had spent the better part of a day aboard his newly acquired fiberglass catboat, and I had tried to share with him what I hoped would be helpful hints. Mostly, we talked about the importance of reefing, and I described how I'd learned the hard way that the time to reef is when one first begins to think about it, no later.

155

Bowling along in a fresh breeze off Naushon Island is Judy, *a 25-foot 6-inch catboat built by Daniel Crosby in 1927.* Judy *has proved to be a particularly able boat, fast and weatherly, and despite her size she is singlehanded regularly by her owner, Ned Kelley. (Stan Grayson photo)*

Lessons like this seem to be best learned from experience, however, for the gentleman in question promptly tried to sail his boat home the following day without a reef in winds of at least 25 knots—singlehanded. He quickly found the boat uncontrollable, anchored, and put in a single reef when he really needed two. He continued his trip, and remembers being a bit scared at times. His chief impression, however, was that the experience "gave me confidence in the boat."

This is a good time, perhaps, to try to define just what catboats are and are not. They are big, roomy boats for their length, and an 18-foot, 2,500-pound fiberglass catboat has little in common with an 18-foot, 900-pound daysailing sloop. In terms of accommodations and performance, the catboat is better compared to a 22- or 23-footer.

Catboats are wonderful vessels for coastal cruising and daysailing, especially in the bays and sounds where they have proved themselves for so many years. Eighteen- and 20-footers have frequently been sailed all along the New England coast, from Connecticut to Maine. The ingenuity applied to these catboats by their owners has to be seen to be appreciated. Catboat owners are able to cover the same waters as those in larger yachts costing far more but usually lacking the catboat's inherent charm and shallow-draft advantages.

Catboats are not primarily passagemakers, nor should they be thought of as ocean cruisers, something oddly tempting to many because the boats are so seakindly and impart a feeling of size and security out of all proportion to their

Attesting to the popularity of fiberglass catboats is this lineup of Marshall 18-footers at Beaton's boatyard in Mantoloking. The boats seen here are only a portion of the large fleet stored each year at Beaton's. (Stan Grayson photo)

actual dimensions. But one need only stand in the enormous cockpit of a big catboat, capable of holding some 15 people, to imagine it being filled by a breaking sea. Neither is the long boom handy when trimmed outboard, where it might catch a sea. That is one reason why some cruising catboaters own a storm trysail or storm jib, either of which can be set under adverse conditions with the boom firmly secured in the crutch. Catboats were never designed for deep-sea sailing, and, although the boats have often proved themselves tremendously able in heavy weather, an ocean passage would tempt fate and prove little. Old-time fishermen apparently did it, but then it was a matter of economic survival, and they understood their boats and the weather in a way few of today's weekend skippers could comprehend.

One who did tempt fate was yacht designer C.P. Kunhardt, whose adventure was referred to in Chapter 1. He sailed his Great South Bay 21-footer 1,600 miles from New York to North Carolina and back, living aboard for eight months. He slept ashore only twice, gained 20 pounds, and viewed the voyage's conclusion with the sentiment that, alas, all good things must end. The cruise demonstrated, he wrote, "what can be done in a small boat only 21 feet long, providing the master is sufficiently expert in her handling and exercises good judgment." But Kunhardt advised others against such a cruise in a boat like *Coot*, because he felt that the cat rig is not as adaptable to open-water work as one that carries a headsail.

One of the most sensible summations of catboat sailing was published in 1907 in a *Boating* magazine article written by William Lambert Barnard. "Every type of

The enormously long boom of a racing catboat is nowhere better shown than in this photograph of C.C. Hanley's Dartwell, *a boat said to have been potentially faster than* Almira. Dartwell's *black spruce mast was 40 feet long and weighed 890 pounds. The 40-foot boom weighed 200 pounds, but the 27-foot gaff was hollow to save weight aloft. "When we had to reef her," said her onetime owner Gus F. Neuberger, "we set up the windward topping lift and somebody had to crawl out on the boom, which extended close to 15 feet beyond the taffrail."* Dartwell *was just over 30 feet long and had an underhung rudder when first launched. Later, to compete in Class D of the Massachusetts Bay Catboat Association, her stern was shortened by 13 inches and the barndoor rudder was installed. Neuberger said* Dartwell *was well balanced, and her best point of sailing was to windward. (Courtesy Wayne Blake and the Mystic Seaport Museum)*

boat, every rig, has its peculiarities. This is particularly true of the cat boat. Her skipper needs to be her master in fact, as well as name, for she has to be managed in every sense of the word. One who receives his training in this type may confidently step from her helm to that of any other fore-and-aft rigged boat and speedily find himself at home. But one born and bred in a sloop or schooner often finds himself completely at the mercy of a cat boat."

What catboat sailor cannot remember his learning experiences? Raising or lowering the big sail so that it neither binds at the gaff jaws nor becomes entangled with lazyjacks or topping lift can take practice. Then there is the prospect of jibing in anything more than a light breeze. Most memorable of all, however, is the sinking feeling that comes from having too much sail hoisted for the weight of wind, and the determined way an overcanvased catboat develops weather helm. The boat takes charge and begins going where *it* wants to, not where you want it to. This business of reefing is of overriding importance to catboat sailing. There are subtleties to making a catboat go, teasing halyards or outhauls or trimming the sheet, but understanding reefing in all its aspects remains central because one cannot shorten sail on a catboat merely by taking in a jib or mizzen. There's just the one sail, and the skipper had better understand how to handle it under different wind conditions. The difference will be a choice between a helm that is barely if at all controllable with two strong arms, and a docile helm that can be tended by one unstrained hand, or even two *fingers*.

Writing in *Yachting* magazine in 1933, Hiram Hamilton Maxim, the proud owner of a 24-foot Crosby-built catboat that spread 675 square feet of sail, wrote: "As I gained experience, both first and second hand, I realized more and more that *Black Duck* possessed qualities which far surpassed even the expectation of my most enthusiastic moments. I learned that, properly handled and rigged, all the disadvantages attributed to the catboat disappeared. I state this without qualification. Sail trim and cut, ballasting, all play important, if not always well understood roles in catboat sailing."

Here is how Maxim reefed his boat:

"First, we set up the topping lift fairly snug to support the boom. Then, lower away on the peak until the gaff is nearly horizontal, with most of the leech flapping in the wind. We then bring her hard on the wind, getting in the mainsheet at the same time. This is done rather slowly so that she will not go over on the other tack. As she comes up and luffs, the mainsheet is got in hard and made fast and the helm is lashed hard down. She loses headway and then falls off almost broadside to the wind and sea, where she will stay indefinitely without any roll to speak of. The weather boom tackle is then snapped on and the boom pulled over into the crutch and the tackle set up taut. She is now all lashed fast and ready for you to get to work on the reef points. The tack is next lashed, after lowering away on the throat, and the two outhaul tackles, one on each side of the boom, are hooked in to the outhaul cringles, which are now hanging just above the stern. The sail may then be hauled out taut, the reef points tied in as usual, and the throat hoisted away. The boom is next let go out of the crutch and the peak set up. The topping lift is slacked off, and you are on your way again. I have accomplished these maneuvers, single-handed many times, with no trouble. With two, the process is a little quicker, taking about fifteen minutes, even in a rather bad blow. With the great wide cockpit and house top you have all the room you want, and never feel as though you might go overboard at any moment."

This reefing method bears study and thought. Except for the boom tackle, it is similar, if not identical, to the reefing methods most catboat sailors will still find useful. Maxim does not mention where he placed his centerboard during this procedure. As a general rule, leaving the board halfway down will keep the boat headed up somewhat yet not promote an inadvertent tack. But board position will vary according to individual boats and is something each sailor needs to experiment with. Maxim also lashed his wheel. Again, some boats will do just fine with the helm left to tend itself. Finally, Maxim noted that he used his boom crutch while reefing. Most catboaters, however, tend to haul in the sheet and cleat it so that the boom is over the quarter. If one has a boom crutch positioned on the quarter, rather than amidships, a position that would tend not to keep the boat on a given tack, then the crutch can be used while reefing.

Discussion of reefing technique is such a popular topic each year at Catboat Association meetings that Ned Kelley once told me he was thinking of having a film made as he went step by step through the reefing of his *Judy*. Kelley has pointed out how much easier he finds reefing when the engine is not used to drive the boat into the wind. "It's easier to put in a reef when underway, under sail, than it is when tied to a dock. Because [when you're underway] all the reef points are sitting right out there: There's no chance of tying in a second point when you're doing all the first points. Everything is easy. You're sitting there just wallowing in a trough, and really, it's exciting."

A big wooden catboat like *Judy*, however, is bound to be steadier when "wallowing" than a fiberglass 18-footer. That is one reason why it's often easier to tie in a reef on a smaller catboat at the dock, being careful not to mix up reef points as you go. Whether one finds it preferable to reef such a boat while lying in the troughs of waves or while moving slowly ahead under outboard power will be, for most, a matter of experimentation. On outboard-powered boats, extreme care must be taken that the sheet does not foul the motor when reefing or heaving-to or at any other time.

The outhauls Maxim had rigged on *Black Duck* were necessary because, like many catboats of her era, *Black Duck*'s boom overhung the transom. The booms are not that long on today's fiberglass boats, but reefing is still quicker, safer, and easier if one fits permanently reeved outhauls at the sail's clew. These should lead through pad eyes and cheek blocks on the boom and belay to an easily reached cleat, also on the boom. It is essential that the sail be stretched tightly along the foot, or else the reefed sail will show wrinkles and will not perform as efficiently as it otherwise might.

A catboat's performance when reefed will vary somewhat. Generally, if the skipper has matched his sail area to the amount of wind, the performance under one or two reefs will be an improvement over what it would be with too much sail on. Many new catboat owners are surprised to find that their boats sail as fast with a reef in as they do under whole sail. When reefed, however, particularly in rough seas, catboats seldom go to windward very well, and such conditions certainly are not their strong point. Reaching or running performance usually remains entirely acceptable.

Most catboats require reefing when the wind exceeds 15 to 18 knots, about the time when a sloop or cutter might be reducing its headsail. For some reason, most catboat sailors never cease to be amazed at the beneficent effects of a reef. It is hard to say where this sense of wonder comes from, but one can pretty surely attribute it to relief, and the pleasure of once again sailing at the modest angle of heel at which a catboat is happiest.

"The effect of the reef is astonishing," wrote Maxim, "as several things are accomplished in one operation. The area of the sail is reduced, the center of pressure is brought in much nearer to the centerline of the boat and the lee bow is not pressed so deeply into the water, all conspiring to make her as easy as can be."

The sloppy alternative to reefing, but no replacement for it, is to scandalize the sail, taking up on the topping lift and then slacking away the peak halyard until the boat is eased. Usually, it helps somewhat to slack the throat a bit, too. Scandalizing works best when sailing off the wind. Going to windward, the slacked sail flaps with a disconcerting din. Still, if the wind increases suddenly and without warning, and you do not intend to drop the sail altogether and resort to power, a scandalized sail is good insurance.

August 1893. The half-decked catboat Dux *carries a party of six for a gentle sail among Boston Harbor islands. (Nathaniel L. Stebbins photo. Courtesy of The Society for the Preservation of New England Antiquities)*

None of today's catboat builders offers really adequate rigging as standard equipment. Whether this is done through ignorance or as a cost-saving measure, the result is the same: The boats are more difficult to handle than they need be. Besides reefing pendants, lazyjacks should be rigged to keep the sail from spilling overboard when lowered. A readily adjustable topping lift on *both* sides of the sail permits the boom to be raised above rough seas without spoiling the sail's draft, regardless of which tack the boat might be on. Topping lifts and lazyjacks should be

The lofty rigs of these two decked catboats must have made them fine performers in light air. Vision's barndoor rudder contrasts with the underhung rudder of the catboat in her lee. (Nathaniel L. Stebbins photo. Courtesy of The Society for the Preservation of New England Antiquities)

positioned so they are easy to reach but don't foul the end of the gaff when the sail is hoisted or lowered. A block rigged at the outhaul is a luxury allowing easily adjustable tension along the sail's foot. This sort of rigging may mean 20 or more fittings on the boom, but such equipment, once common on catboats, makes for a better vessel.

There are few other generalities to be made about catboat sailing. The fine points of handling a catboat are best learned from experience. The most common error newcomers make is to overtrim the sheet, particularly when beating to windward. This is especially damaging to the performance of wooden catboats, which, as a rule, like to be sailed somewhat slacker than most would guess. The fiberglass boats, which usually have sails that peak quite high, are less sensitive, but, like any boat, they too can suffer from overtrimming.

The simplicity of the catboat is there, but it is a simplicity that must be learned, just as a catboat sailor would need to learn about the complexities of genoa tracks and spinnaker gear and, of course, winches, those expensive clicking labor-savers one usually encounters aboard modern boats and some not so modern, but almost never aboard a catboat.

Despite their many fine qualities, catboats have been the subject of myth and misinformation almost since the days when the sloop rig began to be popular. Although there have most certainly been unsuccessful catboats, much criticism of the type was essentially nonsense. It was bandied about, noted a veteran Cape Cod catboat skipper, by men who "didn't know the first thing about catboats." For years, this same old fisherman had singlehanded an engineless Crosby catboat fitted with the enormous sail typical of unpowered working cats. The patience, skills, and understanding peculiar to that sort of sailing began to dwindle with the wide adoption of gasoline engines.

In the book *Sailing Craft*, Edwin Schoettle included a quote from a yachting critic of the 1880s: Catboats, the critic said, are "a bad school for young sailors, a risky one for old—as, in any sea, the heavy mast stepped forward causes the bow to plunge dangerously: in addition, the rig is usually too light to go through rough water, too ungovernable off the wind, and has too much of a tendency for steering wild to make it a safe pleasure craft."

Schoettle answered this attack by recounting how his racing catboat *Scat* had been singlehanded "from Larchmont, New York, thirty miles down the East River, through Hell Gate and New York Harbor to Sandy Hook, and then on the ocean 100 miles to Atlantic City. [The sailor] knew nothing of the lay of the land, was without charts, had the boat loaded with extra spars on deck, three extra sails stored in the cabin, and a rowboat in tow. Despite this handicap and the fact that he was caught in a storm on the ocean and was three days going from Sandy Hook to Atlantic City, he made port with boat and cargo in good shape."

Considering the many hundreds, or thousands, of catboats built through the years, generalizing about them is a risky business. But opinions such as that quoted by Schoettle have little to do with a properly designed, properly handled catboat.

"Take a cat that's pretty full aft and sharp forward and with an excessively big sail, and she'll go out of control when pressed hard," Fenwick Williams pointed out. "But take a boat like *Cimba* [one of Williams's 25-footers], she doesn't steer hard." Williams once wrote a series of articles on catboat design. These were published in *The Catboat Association Bulletin*, and when they were complete, Williams remarked that, somewhat to his own surprise, the design of something as apparently simple as a catboat really was not so simple after all.

It has often been said that genius is the skill for making the difficult appear easy. The baseball player adept at hitting, with no apparent effort, a major league

Rocket is unusual for her great flare at the bow and hollow waterline. (Henry Peabody photo. Courtesy of The Society for the Preservation of New England Antiquities)

curveball, has developed a certain genius not shared by other ballplayers. The same is true of the man who designs outstanding catboats, and, to a much lesser degree, those who have mastered the sailing of them. John Killam Murphy, who owned five catboats during his lifetime, had this to say about catboats and their critics: "There is an almost universal opinion that a catboat must necessarily have a heavy weather helm. Most cats certainly do: but two of my five cats had just as easy a helm as any sloop, yawl, or schooner."

I do not know when or why negative speculation about catboats began to circulate. A plausible time would be those years during which the great racing catboats, having passed through the hands of their original, wealthy owners and professional skippers, were acquired by new owners who thought to sail them without the jibs necessary to balance their outsized sail plans. These boats would have begun changing hands in the very early 1900s, so that, by the time Winfield Thompson wrote an article called "I Buy an Old Cat" in 1911, the catboat's reputation was already miscast in some circles.

"Ever notice how keen most chaps are to give an old catboat a bad name?" Thompson wrote. "The defamers speak in general terms, chiefly on hearsay. Let them have in mind a particular old cat and then hear them linger over the painful details! By the time they have done talking, you are expected to believe there never was a worse boat than that particular old cat, and never a worse type than the class to which she belongs."

Consider *Almira*. This great catboat, built in 1890, passed through a succession of wealthy owners only to drop from sight and reappear in 1906. At that time, she was entered in the Quincy Yacht Club's famous D class. Although *Almira* had originally carried a jib set on a long bowsprit, the Ds were permitted mainsail only. Erling Debes, Hanley's friend and a regular crewmember on the boat, remembered that *Almira* "was very poorly balanced with only her large mainsail."

She was sold, having no more success of course, and in 1912 was acquired by Doctor H. A. Jones, who found her "practically unmanageable due to bad balance." Jones took the boat back to Hanley for the modifications necessary now that she was to sail purely as a catboat. They reballasted the boat, made a new, high-peaked sail, and rerigged the gaff to keep it from bending. Debes remembered that *Almira*'s subsequent vast success helped undo catboat racing around Boston.

"As rebuilt and refined, the *Almira* could out-point and out-foot any Cat Boat she was ever sailed against, and in very light airs she could outsail and outdrift almost any craft, but being at the time 26 years old and having been raced hard for years, she was badly strained and had to have extensive repairs made to her bow in way of the heavy spar."

The oft-forgotten point to keep in mind here is that one cannot alter an important element of a catboat without making compensatory changes elsewhere. A reduction in sail area will require an adjustment in ballast. Some changes—a cut-down centerboard, for example—may forever hamper a boat's windward or tacking ability. Most wooden catboats have undergone substantial modifications by now, to change them from pure sailing boats to sailing auxiliaries, or from racing yachts to cruising yachts, or from cruising yachts with large sails to cruising yachts with smaller sails. Few boats, however, benefited from the systematic modifications Dr. Jones and Hanley provided *Almira*. Perhaps, between 1906 and 1912,

This Fenwick Williams 21-footer, Tambourine, *was built by Bud McIntosh and is owned by Wayne and Irene Blake. The rudder-mounted outboard was successful but has been replaced by a one-cylinder Universal. (Courtesy Wayne Blake)*

Almira was subjected to just the sort of criticism dismissed by Winfield Thompson.

Wooden catboats of 18 to 22 feet or so that have not been hopelessly butchered can become practical, safe, thoroughly enjoyable cruisers for a couple. So can several of the available fiberglass models. Somewhat larger catboats, say, 23 to 26 feet, offer more room and comfort, but their gear is just heavy enough that prospective purchasers might want to consider whether they are up to the labor of raising the sail and carrying out general maintenance. A 25-foot catboat is a substantial yacht.

Just how able a catboat can be when sailed by one familiar with the type was illustrated some 30 years ago in a *Yachting* magazine article by James S. Pitkin. He recalled the following encounter during a trip he made as crewmember aboard a 30-foot yawl in Narragansett Bay.

"Presently, as we surmounted the hissing crest of a towering sea, I saw for an instant, through the mist and flying spray, a mast and a bit of fluttering sail a short distance off to port. Obviously a small boat in distress. While we wallowed through the trough, I recalled the heroic selections I had read concerning the unwritten laws of the sea, the fraternity among seamen, the willingness to risk all in an effort to save. Binoculars in hand, and wondering vaguely who would eventually save whom [for the yawl was making heavy going of the rough seas], I braced myself as we rose again. And then I saw a man in oilskins resting a lobster-pot on the coaming of a Cape Cod catboat! He waved genially and turned back to his work, while we continued on our floundering way."